The Three Secrets of Aging

A Radical Guide

(Pssssst - It Ain't Over Yet)

The Three Secrets of Aging

A Radical Guide
(Pssssst - It Ain't Over Yet)

Rev. John C. Robinson, Ph.D., D.Min.

Foreword by Arjuna Ardagh
The Translucent Revolution

BOOKS

Winchester, UK
Washington, USA

First published by O-Books, 2012
O-Books is an imprint of John Hunt Publishing Ltd., Laurel House, Station Approach,
Alresford, Hants, SO24 9JH, UK
office1@o-books.net
www.o-books.com

For distributor details and how to order please visit the 'Ordering' section on our website.

ISBN: 978 1 78099 040 8

A CIP catalogue record for this book is available from the British Library.

Design: Lee Nash

Printed in the UK by CPI Antony Rowe
Printed in the USA by Offset Paperback Mfrs, Inc

We operate a distinctive and ethical publishing philosophy in all
areas of our business, from our global network of authors to
production and worldwide distribution.

CONTENTS

Foreword

by Arjuna Ardagh
Author: *The Translucent Revolution*

The term 'baby boomer' refers to the population bubble born soon after the Second World War. Many young men in America and Europe had gone off to fight between 1939 and 1945, and not all returned. For those who did, their priorities were clear: settle down, marry your sweetheart, rebuild ... and procreate.

The baby boomer generation officially begins in 1946, but of course not every soldier returning from war was immediately ready to impregnate his sweetheart. Many needed a few years to put a job and house and some savings in place. So the majority of baby boomers were actually born in the 1950s. By 1964 the procreation party was over. If you're born after that year, you qualify more for for the 'X generation' label.

Many massive changes in the way that we live together have been defined by what stage of life those baby boomers find themselves in. In 1967, for example, baby boomers were in their late teens and early 20s. They rebelled, grew their hair, took LSD, and so the adolescence of one generation defined a global social movement.

By that same token, in the late '70s and early '80s, boomers were settling down, having kids, building security. And so these years are characterized by our interest in manifesting, in creating. These are the years of the the EST Seminar, the rise of Tony Robbins.

By the '90s, boomers were in their 40s and early 50s. They had left behind the idealism of their hippy years and the wild entrepreneurism of their 30s. It was time for the boomers to invest. By this time almost all the ponytails have been cut off. The VW bus had long been replaced by a Lexis or even a Mercedes. Hence, the '90s was a time of unparalleled economic growth, a fascination with investment, 401Ks and IRAs.

Today, as we enter the second decade of the 21st century, boomers are preparing for their twilight years. Someone born in 1946 turned 65 in 2011, and so aging has become the hot topic. This extraordinarily honest and insightful book by John Robinson is one of many pioneering attempts to understanding the aging process in a new way that is relevant for boomers.

There are two diverse views which have become popular about aging in the last years. Both have their indisputable merits, but either one adhered to on its own creates severe imbalance.

The fountain of eternal youth

The boomer generation has always had a knack for thinking outside the box. It did its adolescence on a scale unparalleled in human history. It accomplished its creativity in the same way, and now boomers refuse to accept the standard beliefs about aging.

Some of the questions we see in contemporary books on this subject are: Who says that we have to grow old in the way that our parents did? Who even says that the body has to age in the way that we've accepted as inevitable? Who says the body even has to die at all? What is an "incurable disease?"

These kind of questions have led boomers to an interest in the ancient art of Chi kung, practiced for thousands of years in China, where people live in perfect and robust health, and sexual virility well into their 80s. The science of Ayurveda, with a 5000 year history from India , offers us the vision of physical rejuvenation. This determination by boomers to defy the aging process has made alternative health care into a multi-billion-dollar industry and made supplements like ginseng, acai, goji berries and spirulina sell off the shelves like never before.

There's no doubt that our questioning established beliefs about aging is bearing fruit. I remember doing an interview a few years ago with Barbara Marx Hubbard, who recently turned 81. She has renamed 'menopause' to 'regenopause' and claims that the time of a woman's life after she stops having periods is her most creative, productive and juicy time ever.

When Barbara was diagnosed with a very serious kind of blood cancer about eight years ago, she told me "I just see this as an opportunity to question every thought that comes into my mind. I can't afford the luxury now of an unconscious thought." And sure enough, through this kind of thinking outside the box, Barbara has been able to take herself into complete remission and is at her most vibrant yet at 81.

I heard a similar story from George Leonard, now also in his 80s. When I met George, he was also just recovering, this time from an operation. He shared with me that through the regular practice of Aikido, he feels younger and more vibrant than he did in his 50s.

There are literally millions of people alive today who are questioning and reversing the traditional understanding about aging. But like any other view, this can also become imbalanced. When the desire to question the aging process nudges us too far into a denial of the inevitability of our mortality, we can become ridiculous. For example, in December 2010, Hugh Hefner announces his engagement, at 84 years old, to a young woman of 24, sixty years his junior. The marriage was mostly ridiculed in the press, but it was the "comments" section from readers below the news stories that were more interesting. I read people express scorn, compassion, laughing at old Hughey, but you didn't see too many people holding him up as an example of emotional or spiritual maturity. The same thing has been true of Hollywood stars and rock musicians whose endless investments in Botox, facelifts and tight clothing looks more absurd, even scary, that beautiful or impressive.

The Wisdom of Acceptance

The other movement which we've seen among boomers as they age is the seeming opposite of what we've just explored. It involves the deep acceptance of things as they are. When Ram Dass, the author of *Be Here Now* had his stroke, for example, he spoke of watching the body age, and resting more deeply into a dimension of witnessing and acceptance, a dimension which was never born and could never die. This kind of pure observing, with neither clutching nor pushing away has been called 'awakening'.

We have some historical record of ancient cultures which viewed aging in a very different way than we do today. And in India, for example, around the time that the Mahabharata was written, human life was seen as divided into four stages. The first was called Brahmacharya: it meant to be a student - to learn, to absorb, to study, to fully soak up all of the wisdom which previous generations had to offer. The second stage, Grihastha, roughly between 25 and 50, was one of building and creating. It was a time to marry, to have children, to build a house and a family and a career. The third stage, Vanaprastha, was the period of maintaining, and enjoying all you've created. It's the time to welcome grandchildren, to slow down new projects to sustain existing ones. It was thought of as the time when gray hairs began to appear on the head. The last stage is the most interesting, and it's the one that we've lost connection with in our culture. It's the stage of Sannyasa. Now, completely white headed, the elder abandons all attachment to the world and wanders off into the Himalayas to meditate and live out the rest of his or her days in solitude and silence. We prepare to leave this world in the same way we entered: with empty hands and an empty mind.

Boomers have taken an increasing interest in meditation, in retreat, and in the true meaning of spiritual awakening. This view of course can also be taken out of proportion, like any other, and can become a way of avoiding living out our life to its fullest potential.

Dr. Robinson's book is a prime example of what I would call a "translucent view" of the aging process. It falls neither into one extreme or the other. It allows us to make the very best of our declining years on the planet, but without attachment, or grasping, or making ourselves the objects of ridicule.

I want to leave you in these few pages with a scene that I witnessed many years ago. At the time, my two sons were about six and nine. My friend Pete Russell, who wrote the book *The Global Brain*, came up for the weekend from the Bay Area for a little R & R. On Saturday morning he got out the Monopoly set with the boys, and they got launched into a tournament that went on hours.

I remember at a certain point my youngest son, Shuba, landed his silver top hat or racing car on a square where Pete had two hotels built. Shuba had to pay out almost all his money. He flew into a rage, ran to his room, slammed the door screaming "I hate you all!" It took us 15 minutes to coach him out. Pete, on the other hand, was enjoying the game, not to win or lose, but to relax and have fun. It really made no difference to him what the outcome was, and in fact when my older son came through as the victor, Pete was delighted.

In one sense, this is the essence of aging with wisdom. You still participate fully. You still play the game with gusto. You still build hotels. You still go to jail and wait to roll a double six. But you do all these things in a spirit of amused detachment. If you win, you win; if you lose, you lose; but you've learned that is not the point of being here.

Imagine for a moment that it was Pete, at fifty five, and not Shuba at six, who ran to his room and slammed the door screaming. What would have been the result? You know as well as I do that when he emerged, we would have looked at Pete perhaps with compassion, perhaps with amusement, and also with a little less trust than we had before. If Pete had hysterics over the results of the game, he would have, in a sense, failed the aging test.

As we grow old, the respect of younger generations is not something to which we have any entitlement. It's something we can earn through aging with maturity. We often hear it lamented that so many people die lonely in nursing homes, that their families ignore or forget them. Of course, that is a tragic picture. But you can't blame such a scenario entirely on the younger generations. If an old person's bodily functions begin to fail, but they remain rigidly attached to their beliefs and habits, to their political or religious persuasion, or trying to keep the body younger than it is, they have aged, but they have not become wise.

As baby boomers, we have the opportunity to practice the art of playing to play rather than playing to win. We have the examples of Barbara Marx Hubbard, George Leonard and countless others to give us inspiration. As we learn to be examples of wise, amused, and wide awake consciousness for younger generations, we can earn the respect of those following behind us, and we discover our finest gifts in our twilight hours.

Acknowledgements

To my editor, Tinker Lindsay, for helping me turn a heavily loaded truck into a streamlined sports car. Like her namesake Tinker Bell, she works magic with pixie dust.

To my publisher, John Hunt, who has the courage and vision to publish wisdom beyond the collective myth, knowing that one day it will catch fire and change the world.

To my many "old" friends – you know who you are! We are in this together. Thank you for being with me.

Preface

Why Did I Write This Book?

In a dream some twenty-five years ago, I found myself in a large library. At the top of one bookcase were five golden books. I did not, or could not, read them, I only knew they were filled with a wisdom far beyond my years. I later understood that these were books I might write one day. *The Three Secrets of Aging* is my fifth book.

All my life I have felt as if I were preparing for a great test or responsibility arriving in my later years, as if every course I took, every degree I earned, every spiritual practice I learned, and every wound I healed, readied me for this great challenge. Premonition, fantasy, grandiosity, prophecy? Yet I cannot conceive of a purpose greater or truer than this: Transforming the human experience of aging into spiritual enlightenment in the service of peace on Earth.

My father lost his way in this final stage of life. Once vibrant and masterful, Dad retired early and then slid steadily into alcoholism and depression. He lost his community and his identity. "What is the purpose of life?" he would ask in quiet despair. "What is the role of a father?" and "How should we live?" His asking such profound and searching questions at the family dinner table stimulated my own life-long search for meaning. But now I understand these questions in a new way as central to the experience of aging rather than merely symptoms of depression. They express the hunger of this last stage to grasp what life has been all about. With no cultural or scientific support to pursue his questions, for aging into the 1970's and 80's was greatly misunderstood, my father muddled along uncertainly and died at the age of 75. I went merrily on with my life.

Then aging happened to me. I, too, retired early. I, too, fell under the spell of those same questions and some of the same depression. So I write this book for both of us – to answer his questions for myself and to bring my answers home to him when I die.

My 92-year-old mother is now living in a nursing home sliding ever further into dementia. She had asked me, her second son, to be her executor, her power-of-attorney for health care decisions, and her caregiver. It has been a long and difficult road since my wife and I moved in with her and then, after five long months, collapsed in the exhaustion of caregiver burnout, and moved her into a nursing home. Her life in dementia now poses equally profound though unspoken questions to me. How do we understand the spiritual meaning of dementia at the end of a vital and active life? Prior to her decline, my mother and I often discussed the nature and challenges of old age; now she is showing me a world that transcends language yet I suspect also encodes cryptic answers to these questions. It is for her, too, that I write this book.

I also write this book for myself. I'm getting old and I refuse to do this final stage of life alone and unprepared. As a psychologist, interfaith minister, author, teacher, mystic, and life-long spiritual seeker, I want to apply my understanding and life experience to this journey, to dig deep into its hidden meanings, pitfalls and treasures, and to share my discoveries with others. I am constantly reviewing the literature and exploring the views and opinions of others (devouring scores of books and conversations in the process), searching for insights and conclusions that fit my own "lived" experience. A careful examination, in-depth meditation, and experiment in personal growth, *The Three Secrets of Aging* is how I have chosen to prepare for life's final chapter. Many are lucky enough now to reach old age, but few prepare for it and fewer still understand its secrets. So this book is my way of lighting the path for others.

The good news is, by digging deeply into those areas most of us would rather avoid, I have a new attitude about aging. Being old feels rather good to me now – sometimes exciting, often challenging, but mostly just right, as if it were meant to be exactly the way it is. I now love and give and understand more easily and I believe this comfort can flow into your experience of aging as well. I'd like you to see how sweet and special, yet powerful, it is to be old, to be slow, peaceful, easy-going, patient, kind, and wise, but also fiery with conviction, cleansed with awakened consciousness, and happily helpful to family, friends, and community. In tune with things, in the flow, trusting life to show and lead the way – these are some of the gifts that aging offers to the enlightened Elder and his world, eventually transforming old age, dying and death. I'm excited about sharing with you three radical secrets I've discovered that changed my experience of aging from a time of fear and depression to one of joy and transformation.

Why Read This Book?

Are the realities of aging and death beginning to touch you personally? Perhaps you've already had experience with aging and dying parents or older friends, or wish to have a better understanding of the feelings and problems of someone you love whose aging now concerns you. Do you now wonder what the next twenty years will bring and what your own aging and death will be like? Maybe the physical changes in your aging body, a recent age-related illness, or the way you look in those photos is starting to remind you of time's inevitable action in your life. Are you experiencing uncomfortable doubts, fears, and regrets associated with growing old? Do you feel a need to look at what this time of life involves and consider how best to handle the hard parts? You are wise to do so. The sooner you start, the more prepared you will be.

The Three Secrets of Aging explores the psychology, spirituality and mysticism of life's final chapters. While the *psychological* dimension of aging has been addressed by countless writers, I include it here to examine how identity, loss and change under-write our unfolding spiritual and mystical evolution. When I refer to the *spiritual* dimension of aging, I am not talking about formal religious beliefs but rather the personal intuitions that arrive spontaneously in the aging process – universal realizations of meaning and purpose applicable to all people and religions. By introducing the *mystical* dimension of aging – those remarkable experiences of ultimate reality that completely transform our understanding of life – I am intentionally inviting the sacred into our discussion, honoring its profound influence in our final years.

The astonishing truth is, these psychological, spiritual, and mystical forces, deeply embedded in the aging process, are already stirring unexpected and often extraordinary possibilities in the psyche and spirit of today's Elder. All we need to do is call them forth. By uncovering your own experience and intuition, you will be writing your own book on the spirituality of aging, personally and perfectly relevant to your own aging situation. That way, however the journey proceeds, it will be *your* journey. As the dying Buddha told his disciples, "Be a light unto yourself."

I also want to make reading this book a deeply valuable experience, even if it is about a difficult topic. I'll strive to keep the writing as clear, relevant, and easy to read as possible, avoiding jargon and academic hair-splitting, and I promise to always hold you, the reader, in my heart and mind as we take this journey together. I honor you for the courage to grow psycholog-ically, spiritually and mystically in the classroom of aging.

This book may not be for everyone. It is not for people who want to believe that aging can be conquered with exercise, nutrition, and positive thinking, and assume that they will simply die peacefully in their sleep. This book is for people who desire to face aging and death with honesty, dignity, humor, and wisdom, and in the process, be ready and grateful for all that will be revealed. Aging has no "solution"; rather, it is a river of experience through a mysterious land. The more we can share our experiences and support one another, the more we can understand, accept, and surrender to this final transformation. At times difficult, fun, surprising, painful, and amazing, aging asks us to stay involved, keep learning, and prepare for circumstances never before imagined. Are you with me?

Summing Up

This book is not an academic study of aging – aging observed from the outside with statistics, methodology, or theories; it's about aging from the inside, tapping into our deepest hopes, potentials, intuitions, and unfolding psychological, spiritual and mystical realizations. And the wisdom of age does not come easily. I wrote *The Three Secrets of Aging* over ten hard and turbulent years, knowing that I could not rush the kinds of insights that only germinate with time, struggle, and sometimes terrible loss. Real wisdom is often earned the hard way – through mistakes, foolishness, tragedies, and the healing power of love. This book is for those of us who are willing to be pioneers of a new awareness, who understand that aging and death are meant to expand our consciousness, grow our soul, and increase our ability to love, forgive, surrender, and meet death head on.

While none of us know how our own aging experience will turn out, I am grateful that you are here. Whatever happens, by the time we arrive at the end of the book, I am confident that something new and profound will have been discovered, understood, or revealed for both of us. I begin with a mixture of excitement, dread, hope and wonder. How do you feel? Are you ready? Buckle your seat belts, we're in for an amazing ride. Thanks for coming with me.

Introduction

The Challenge of Aging

Hey, boomers, we're aging! Our bodies are changing, energy's lagging, youthful looks are fading (or long gone!). Ever notice that you're often one of the oldest people in a room now? Face it, the accumulated years have begun to reconfigure body, mind and spirit, and the hands on this clock cannot be turned back. Awesome, scary, relentless and mysterious, aging will not be denied. We're getting old.

I was born in 1946, the first official year of the boomer wave, so I may be further down the road than some of you. And what I and my older friends are experiencing is startling: Physical energy, athletic skills, and sexual drive have diminished considerably (I'm only a legend in my own mind now); we play hide-and-seek with car keys and glasses (where did I leave them?); everyday words, the names of family and friends, and even simple intentions fall through the sieve of memory ("What was I looking for?"); soft voices disappear in noisy restaurants ("It's not my hearing, you're mumbling!"); the fine print is harder to read ("When did those instructions get smaller?"), and prescription medications are now a daily fact ("I'm up to three now; whoops, make that four, how about you?"). To make matters worse, the values, dress, and vocabulary of the young seem ever more inexplicable, the sheer number of young people rushing God-knows-where texting (or is it sexting?) astounds me, and social media sites have replaced old-fashioned conversation. I never expected aging to be quite like this, though I don't really know what I did expect, and my older friends hint at much more to come. Boomers, I can tell you, aging is beginning to happen for real. What are we to do?

At first we confidently proclaim, "No problem!" Having spent all our lives seeking love, knowledge, fortune, truth, self, and

God, aging should be cakewalk. After all, we've mastered career, finances, science, technology, civil rights, holistic medicine, organic gardening, the Internet, and spirituality. Ten thousand self-help books taught us to manage time, achieve our dreams, eat healthy, meditate, get rich, run marathons, locate the "G" spot, know the self, and discover inner peace. We don't settle for the given, we seek the possible and sometimes even the impossible. And because we are living in a time of exponential change – and living longer – it seems like anything we can conceive should be attainable. In sum, our life-long project of self-improvement can simply continue onward into the sunset. Right? Wrong!

We, whose life purpose was to build the best résumé, have perfect children, and wind up with the most toys, must instead face a progressive unraveling of this whole enterprise. We can't take it with us. We can't even keep it together. Sooner or later we realize that the *project of me* will fail. Physical and economic decline, the deaths of friends and family, and the cultural disempowerment of the aged will systematically dismantle the U.S.S. Enterprise of Self. Sooner or later, our whole world will come apart.

But wait! There must be a way out of this mess. For us boomers, there is a solution to every problem. After all, we have a long and proud history of trading in old paradigms for new and better ones: traditional religion gave way to New Age spirituality (then we rediscovered traditional religion), sexual prohibition was replaced by the sexual revolution, typewriters morphed into computers and computers became smart phones, and gender stereotypes were shattered by the women's and men's movements. We were the radical generation, the nonconformists. We lived life differently. We grew our hair long, staged sit-ins, burned draft cards (and bras), sought enlightenment, blew our minds on psychedelics, and wouldn't trust anyone over thirty. It ain't over til it's over. Think outside the box.

There must be a solution to aging.

Indeed, the avalanche of books on growing old spring from this same, ever-inspiring, boomer denial. The reader is encouraged to overcome aging (and perhaps even death) through nutrition, exercise, social activity, prayer, yoga, attitude, financial and retirement planning, growth hormones, cosmetic surgery, trendy fashions, the latest scientific knowledge, and maybe even cryogenics. The constant and reassuring message is this: re-invent yourself and extend your well-oiled identity indefinitely into the future. Hey, octogenarians are doing iron man marathons! Ninety is the new 50! Of course we'll conquer aging. Just stay tuned.

Death of the Hero (Again!)

I hate to crash the party but let's look at facts: Sooner or later gainful employment ends, income levels drop, personal appearance erodes, health declines, senses fail, and the relentless social, cultural, and technological changes driven by younger generations will completely replace the world you know. We are growing old and the *project of me* is destined to crumble like a house of cards. First we're replaced. Then we die. It happens to everyone, always has, and always will. Aging wins. We don't need studies and statistics to see what's right in front of us: old people are old! They are not the same as young people.

My first book was about the Midlife Passage. *Death of a Hero, Birth of the Soul* argued that the traditional drive for mastery and conquest needed to be put aside at midlife so the unfolding of the soul can take place. This book goes even further, suggesting that the challenge of growing old is not to conquer aging but to enter a natural, meaningful, and profoundly transforming process – an evolutionary agenda in which the whole *project of me* dissolves into an entirely new consciousness and way of life. This final developmental stage, which I have called the *Late Life Passage*, can neither be controlled nor overcome, but it can – if you'll trust it –

transform and complete your journey on Earth. While our Midlife Passage crosses the divide between the first and second halves of life, the *Late Life Passage* of aging crosses a developmental threshold previously unknown in human history (few lived long enough to study it!). We step into a brand new world.

Now, for most of us, the idea of surrendering the *project of me* seems either inconceivable or plain ridiculous. After all, how do we let go of something we've devoted forty, fifty, even sixty years to believing, defending, and improving? I am now virtually an institution! But in reality, surrender is not only inevitable, it embodies a deep natural confluence of biological, psychological, spiritual and mystical forces drawing us into a new evolutionary stage of consciousness.

The Disguise of Age

Staring at a recent photograph of myself, I wonder, "Who is this person that looks so old? When did this 'old man' disguise appear and who put it there? Did some Hollywood make-up artist slip into my room unnoticed while I was sleeping and make me look so different? I know the disguise is not the real me, but where did that person go and how do I remove the makeup?" Worse yet, younger people (and they all seem younger now) only seem to see the disguise. They call me "sir," watch intently for signs of frailty, senility or incompetence, then largely ignore me as another species irrelevant to their lives.

And it all seems so unfair. On the inside, I feel no more than 30 years old (OK, maybe 40). Despite those now-familiar aches, pains, and physical limitations that apparently came with the disguise, I should be easily understood and accepted by – and even attractive to! – all those other 30 and 40-year-olds. But all they see is an older man, invisible and insignificant. Does this sound familiar to you?

The Miracle of Life-Long Transformation

Do not despair. Something very different is going on behind the disguise of age: life's never-ending miracle of transformation. The truth is our appearance in photographs has changed every year from birth on. Do you look or feel like a newborn infant, 7-year-old scout, testing teenager, determined young adult, or middle-aged worker? In the past, we viewed these changes as signs of progress and even thought them pretty cool. Well, this same miracle is still changing our body, mind, identity, and beliefs only now it's called aging. We are being changed yet again and it's still meaningful and exciting. The real question is, "What's going on behind the disguise?" The answer is, "A lot!"

Behind every "old-person" disguise hide three secret and powerful psychospiritual processes: *initiation, transformation, and revelation.* Aging is an *initiation* into a new and extraordinary stage of life, a profound *transformation* of self and consciousness, and the *revelation* of Heaven on Earth all around us. Each process brings profound challenges but, to the prepared, equally profound gifts. These three radical secrets of aging can completely rewrite our story of growing "old." And why not? Why shouldn't the miracle of aging be as amazing as the miracles preceding it?

Understanding the three secrets of aging will revolutionize your Late Life Passage, not by executing a clever end-run around the facts and experiences of growing old – that would be just another boomer-like denial – but by diving deeply into the experience. We will not avoid the "Road of Trials" that is old age but we can redeem the pain for far greater treasures.

Warning!

The three secrets of aging – initiation, transformation, and revelation – may generate painful and disorienting experiences, especially if we resist them! Everything you believe and count on can disappear overnight in the aging process, sometimes erasing all the familiar landmarks of our life. But remember, loss and hardship often precede great transformations (remember how much we grew and learned from previous losses, like failed relationships, frustrating jobs, or broken dreams?). A core assumption of this book is that we grow psychologically, spiritually, and mystically only in so far as we are willing to accept change, work on our self, and strive to find the next step on a pathless path. Keep in mind also that this book is not just another self-improvement project; rather it invites the reader to experience an extraordinary consciousness in which the whole idea of self-improvement disappears as well. From this consciousness flow revelations that would never come from the *project of me*.

Doing It for Yourself, You Do It for the World

We are living in dangerous times – terrorism, war, pollution, greed, failing economies, poverty, climate damage, cyber attacks, mutating viruses, food and water shortages – that may soon threaten our very existence. The old boomer success model, with its emphasis on competition, progress, and acquisition – not to mention iconoclasm and radical cultural deconstruction – now infects the whole world, contributing heavily to these global problems. *The Three Secrets of Aging* offers an antidote to this rapidly-spreading illness. It suggests that aging in the twenty-first century can herald a completely new stage of human evolution, one that holds the key to our future on Earth, if we understand and embrace it.

The "happy fantasy" approach to aging – images of golf, retirement villas, and dancing to golden oldies – will not solve the problem of physical decline nor will it benefit our children and the world we leave them. The gifts we offer each other and future generations depend on *how* we age now. So, let us discover together what these three secrets of aging have to teach us. No matter how old you are, how deep in the transformational flow of the aging experience, it is never too late to apply these secrets. They may help us understand and reframe what is already happening and give our aging, and its problems, new meaning. It's a matter of choice. You will not become an enlightened Elder just by getting old. You must choose this journey or it probably won't happen. This is the "Road Less Traveled." Doing it for myself; I do it for the world.

Finally, let this book change you. I humbly offer it as a new synthesis of the potential psychological, spiritual, and mystical dimensions of aging. Its ultimate realizations may seem unbelievable at first, for until now, only the greatest sages have traveled this far. But we are already following in their footsteps. I believe the aging experience described here can eventually become the path to a collective transformation and the discovery of a new world.

The Three Secrets of Aging is divided into two parts. Part I, a memoir, describes my discovery of the secrets. Part II explains each secret in detail so you will be better able to understand and apply them to your aging experience. The appendices supply additional elucidation on particular subjects. My hope is that this mix of memoir and explanation will meaningfully inform and empower your aging experience.

One last piece of advice. Don't rush through this book. You have more time now, take it! The journey of aging should stay new and fresh over time because the most important insights will come from you. Put another way, the material presented here will always be current and relevant if you apply it sincerely. This isn't something to digest in one sitting, but rather to experience over time, to savor again and again. Your depth of understanding will evolve with every passing year. As Carl Sagan said, it takes a whole universe to create an apple pie, so it should come as no surprise that it takes a whole life to understand *The Three Secrets of Aging*. Finally, the vision in this book may seem ahead of the culture's collective view of aging. If you are reading this, however, it means that you, too, are ahead of that curve and already well into its three secrets. And that means you will have much to do and contribute.

Part I. Coming Into Age

Part I is a story of aging, my own aging – a memoir of a long and difficult journey from middle age to old age. It is a story of defeat, failure and deconstruction; of loss, grief and death; of discovery, change and renewal; of initiation, transformation and revelation. Both unique and universal – there are elements unlike any you may ever experience and elements common to all of us, it is a story of enlightenment hidden in the journey of aging. This story is my gift to you. May it light your path to wisdom and happiness.

Part I

Coming Into Age

Initiation

In so many ways, the journey of life consists of recurring initiations – each new phase marked by an event or experience of often-unrecognized profundity that forever changes our life. Our first day of school, our first best friend, that driver's license, first sexual experience, high school graduation, leaving home for work, college, or military. Some initiations are celebrated with rituals; most are not. Initiation into aging is no different. It begins with a turning point, a water shed experience or realization, that alters everything. For me, the initiation of aging began when my heart lost its rhythm.

In the spring of 2000, I was a 54-year-old husband, father, and clinical psychologist going about my everyday family and professional life in Sacramento, California. One day, I experienced a most peculiar sensation in my chest. It felt as if there were hands working inside my heart. I imagined this to be God moving within me. A lovely image. But unlike the image, this sensation was not particularly pleasant and would not go away. It was also connected to fear. Why should I be afraid?

Then it struck like the first lightning crack from a summer thunderstorm. At the end of a long workday, I sensed my heart beat becoming irregular and explosive. It felt like a fish flopping wildly inside my ribcage. *Atrial fibrillation*. Recalling a similar episode of a decade earlier, I went to the emergency room to see if my heart had again lost its normal rhythm. It had. An IV of heart regulating medication began. But this time the rhythm did not "convert" to normal. They sent me home with more medication. With no improvement by the next day, *atrial defibrillation* was strongly recommended.

Atrial defibrillation? Isn't that what you see on the TV dramas like ER: "Get the paddles. Stand Back. Clear!" We watch the patient's body bounce on the table as a powerful electrical current shocks the heart. Distracted by these images, I tried to listen as the doctor explained the risk of blood clots and stroke that rises dramatically after 48 hours in a continuously fibrillating heart. Atrial defibrillation, he said, would literally stop my heart beat for a moment with a strong electrical shock to reset its rhythm. Unlike the TV dramas, he reassured me, I would be rendered temporarily unconscious and feel nothing. Yeah, right! Now I was scared.

Resting on a hospital bed in the ER, I talked with my wife, asked the doctor all the questions I could think of, even spoke with a young man whose defibrillating heart rhythm had been converted to normal earlier in the day. And I prayed. After a long hour and a half of emotional preparation, I signed the consent forms and moved to a small operating theater. There I observed the E.R. physician and several nurses prepare the defibrillating equipment. My wife was asked to go to the waiting room. Unbeknownst to the staff, she returned instead and stood silently behind a thin partition, determined to stay close by. A sedative introduced through my IV swept me quickly into unconsciousness. On awakening, I asked immediately, "Am I converted?" and the doctor replied, "Yes, you're Jewish." With this unexpected levity, and a vast – almost giddy – sense of relief, I believed the experience was over.

It wasn't. Soon after coming home, a profound exhaustion overwhelmed me. I was so tired that I could barely go to the office much less listen thoughtfully to my clients. I also sensed that this "heart attack" had been a warning, that if I resumed work as if nothing had happened, I would die. And there was something even more disturbing. A shudder of death – cold and clammy – now haunted my soul. I needed time and distance to sort out what this experience wanted from me.

Renting a small house for a week on the northern California coast, I retreated into myself. For the first three days, I collapsed in the quiet of this remote forest dwelling. Fog drifted up through the redwoods from the ocean and sunlight illuminated the new green tips of redwood branches. I walked the beaches, listened to the surf pound the shore, wandered the headlands, saw beauty everywhere, and ate alone. Silence, solitude, and peace washed over my depleted psyche. Everyday I tried to go deeper into this feeling of a stricken, broken, and wounded heart. What was this all about?

The first answer came quickly. I realize that my heart was tired. As a psychologist with a full and demanding practice, I had been taking care of too many people for too long. Professionals in the field call this compassion fatigue or "burn-out." Years of caring for people in psychological distress had taken their toll. But as I was soon to learn, this was not the whole story.

Still tired upon returning home, I decided to cut my practice back to half time for several months to give myself more space to rest and recover. But I didn't recover. Instead, I begin to feel strange sensations in my chest. Words like rubbery, thick, tingling, and numb came to mind. What was going on? My cardiologist and family doctor each assured me that my heart was fine. One day, it hit me. *I felt as if I had literally just awakened from heart surgery.* How could that be? How could I know what heart surgery felt like? Flash back four decades for an answer.

At the age of 14, I was hospitalized for repair of a "hole in the heart," an abnormal opening in the wall (septum) between the heart's upper chambers first detected at birth as a heart murmur. Referred to as an atrial-septal defect, this congenital abnormality, when serious, can result in a progressively weakened heart and shortened life span. Born in 1946, prior to the advent of open-heart surgery, there was little that could be done for a defect of this magnitude. My mother told me later that doctors had estimated my life expectancy to be somewhere in the mid forties, with significant physical limitations accruing in early adulthood. By 1960, however, open-heart surgery had been successfully performed for several years. It was going to be my turn.

I recall that June well. It was early in the summer before the eighth grade. Physical symptoms had not yet appeared, no one was talking about my heart, so I felt pretty normal and healthy. My pediatrician, however, advised my parents to seek surgical consultation with a cardiac specialist. A heart cathiterization was performed - the doctor inserted a wire into my right arm and threaded it up through my veins into my heart. I watched a TV monitor tracking the wire's jerky snaking movement, a rather erratic process that triggered uncanny physical sensations and occasional heart flutters. When it passed through the "hole" in my heart, the defect was found. Unknown to me, my name was immediately placed on the waiting list for open-heart surgery.

Back home, the summer was still young. Swimming, baseball, hanging out with my brothers and neighborhood friends. Three weeks later, early one morning, the telephone call came. "John, that was the hospital," my mother said. "A boy on the heart surgery schedule for tomorrow got a cold and his operation was postponed. They want you to take his place. We need to pack an overnight bag right away and be there by 2:00." I was numb. Can this really be happening? What will it be like? No one tells me what to expect. My mother drove me to the hospital in San Francisco. Fear mounted rapidly, mine and hers, as the minutes go by. Everyone else on the highway had someplace normal to go. Not me. I was going to the hospital to have my heart opened up. I was too scared to speak. Later my brothers would tell me that they didn't really understand what was happening that day, they only knew it was very serious because dad cooked the dinner that night. No one talked about it.

In the 1960's, little was known about the psychological preparation of children for major surgery. I assumed the staff was trying to be reassuring when they took me up to see the children who have just come out of surgery. All I saw were kids in oxygen tents with scars and tubes and monitors. It was very scary.

Furthermore, parents did not spend the night in the hospital in those days and children received virtually no explanation of the proposed surgery or post-operative experience. No one even asked me how I felt about it. I was a scared 14-year-old boy who couldn't say a word. My mother, it turned out, was just as scared. Her brother, after whom I was named, died of polio at 14! Her fear was enormous. I still get tearful every time I tell this story.

Yet there was going to be even more to this terrifying experience. Also in the 1960's, little was known about the possibility that for some people, the anesthesia might not work completely. In those cases, surgery can be consciously experienced in a state of chemically-induced muscular paralysis, with no way to communicate this horrifying reality. In other words, you can look unconscious but still be awake! Nor was the patient's brain activity monitored with sophisticated equipment. Why should it be? After all, the individual was presumed to be unconscious.

I could not get to sleep the night before surgery. Frightened and alone in a darkened hospital room, I rang for the nurse. I needed emotional comfort, I got a sleeping pill. That's all I remembered until I awoke from surgery in a drugged haze, with adhesive tape running down the center of my chest, a tube exiting my right ribcage into a bottle on the floor, and a cold IV in the top of my hand. My mother peered anxiously through the small window of my room in the Cardiac Intensive Care Unit. My body felt crushed, broken, violated, shocked, profoundly traumatized, as if I'd been hit by a cement truck. When I viewed the scar for the first time, I was horrified. I looked like Frankenstein: cut apart and stitched back together, a monster. My chest also felt bruised on the inside, where it doesn't show, where I cannot even describe it. And I was terrified that the surgical scar would come open again if I moved suddenly or coughed excessively.

Every night, I slept with my hands over my chest, as if I

needed to be sure the wound did not come open. I could feel wires holding the sternum together, their twisted ends poking up through my skin in uncomfortable little bumps. My parents usually visited one at a time in the afternoon. My brothers never came. A week later, I went home.

It took the rest of the summer for me to recover my strength. The months passed slowly. I returned to school. Restrictions were removed one by one. Soon the whole traumatic experience - what could be remembered and what I never remembered - lay deeply buried in my psyche. I also suppressed as much of the experience as I could. What other choice did I have? This was adolescence! I needed to be normal at any cost. Then, miraculously, life resumed as if nothing had happened. But it had.

I graduated from high school, went off to college, discovered psychology, and applied to graduate school, earning my doctorate five years later. After working in a hospital two years, I passed the licensing examinations and began private practice. So much to learn! Career, marriage, fatherhood, divorce, relation-ships, remarriage, blended family – the summer of life was a very busy time.

Fast forward to 2000. Forty years to the month after my open-heart surgery, the electrical shock of defibrillation awakened the entire trauma. What bizarre timing! I felt as if I had once again been surgically opened and sewn shut, literally. As real and intense as the original experience, my chest again felt shattered, fragile, numb, traumatized, and tight. And the strange feeling of hands inside my heart? That's the surgeon! I was re-experiencing the operation itself. Then I recalled a psychologist friend of mine describing his research on awareness in surgery. It hit me like a ton of bricks: "That's what happened to me." Unable to bear the horror of waking up in surgery as a boy, the whole experience had been locked away in countless unfinished body sensations and splintered memories.

It got progressively worse. I began to relive the surgery itself on a daily basis through horrific physical sensations, gruesome dreams, and nightmarish memories. Many times I could barely stand being inside my skin! With the shocking realization of what I had experienced as a boy, and was now having to feel again as a man, came a tsunami of emotional pain. This was no longer an intellectual exercise. I found a psychotherapist. In session after session, an almost unbearable, unnamable, grief poured from my soul. More and more memories surfaced, each with its own quantum of fear, pain, helplessness, rage, and sorrow.

Descending ever deeper into traumatic body memories, I was confronted then with the reality of death. Indeed, it felt as if I had died or been murdered. Looking back, I realize that this conclusion is not unreasonable. During the surgery, the rhythm of my breath and heartbeat - that constant ground of physical existence – was stopped, replaced by a heart-lung machine; my temperature abnormally lowered, my body totally paralyzed, and my chest split open. It was like a living autopsy: I had known the cold shudder of death! Moreover, part of me was still dead: frozen in trauma and disconnected from the rest of my psyche. It was clear then that I had to find this lost and devastated child and bring him back to life.

Finally it all made sense. A delayed *Posttraumatic Stress Disorder* had been triggered. My body and psyche were literally replaying the heart surgery. Eventually, my symptoms became so severe that I closed my practice. If I was to survive this nightmare, I had to give myself completely to this journey of healing. Saying good-bye to patients and colleagues I had known for years, I surrendered my profession.

Thus began my initiation into aging. Arriving earlier than most, it nonetheless embodied all of the familiar themes – a life-changing event or realization; the disorienting loss of identity, community, or career; personal health concerns; questions of meaning, purpose and mortality; and the long process of understanding and accepting this unexpected new life.

Week after week, my therapist acknowledged, validated, and supported my anguish. Given the psychological devastation associated with my surgery experience, he frequently reminded me, this pain made perfect sense. I had been a young adolescent boy exposed to a horrifying experience with neither preparation nor emotional support. The result was a shattering level of trauma and emotional disconnection. My therapist also allowed himself to be moved by my suffering, which helped me find compassion for my own self. Therapy provided both an invaluable container holding me together and an outlet for the enormous grief I had buried inside. I could not hold it by myself. My therapist also became a guide, my Virgil through Dante's Inferno, for I no longer had the strength or vision to chart my own course.

Many other people supported me through the unfathomably painful memories of this trauma. I shared my feelings and discoveries with my wife, family, close friends, and men's group. One of the most poignant experiences came with my mother. I needed to tell her what had really happened forty years ago. Sitting together in her kitchen shortly before her dementia took her away, we cried together – a 55-year-old son and an 83-year-old mother - no guilt, no self-recrimination, just deep acceptance, contact, and love.

The turning point in my healing came when I began to "hold" the devastated 14-year-old boy. Using imagination, I focused my own loving tenderness and concern on the post-surgical boy. At first, his appearance - weak, numb, cold, trembling, and ashen – shocked and saddened me. In fact, the very first image I had was a boy frozen in a block of ice, a powerful and disturbing symbol of my traumatized self. I gradually removed the child from the ice and gently held him, massaging his scalp and face, stroking his hair, putting hot compresses on his chest, neck, and thighs, and talking to him in soothing, reassuring tones. I asked how he felt and what he needed, and listened as he described old and new memories of terror, helplessness, and grief. I reassured this boy that he was OK now, that he had survived, that the nightmare of surgery was finally over, that I loved him, and that he would heal. It was slow going at first but soon the devastated child inside me began to respond.

One day, to my surprise, I sensed the boy had actually moved into my chest. He was no longer split off from me! As I continued holding and comforting him, I could see that he was healing. I could now bear the pain and anguish by myself. I held him as I had never been held. I'll never forget the day I discovered that the boy in my imagination finally looked normal again. I noticed then what a gentle, sensitive, and thoughtful child he was – as I had been before the surgery. He was going to be OK.

Despite my healing, I could not bring myself to resume my profession. I was done. Less a rational decision than an irreversible realization, I knew I could no longer bear the emotional pain of others in the way a psychotherapist must. Something had changed deep inside me. I needed to find another path.

With the ending my career, I struggled for several years wondering what I should do with my life. Prematurely retired, I was no longer Dr. Robinson the psychologist. I was nobody. Identity, colleagues, clients, work, income, and daily routine all fell away. What good was I now? What was I living for? I experienced this emptying as a profoundly painful deconstruction of identity, purpose, and life structure. Remaining in the ashes of my old life had also become unbearable.

It was time for a new adventure. My wife and I left our long-time home in Sacramento and moved with two other couples to the Puget Sound of Washington State looking for a new life. We settled on a rainy and wind-swept island – an incredibly beautiful place, and enjoyed lots of adventures with our friends, traveling and exploring this new area. But it was also isolated here. I felt lonely, bereft, and unsettled.

Sensing that I needed a new beginning, and a new philosophical scaffolding for all I was experiencing, I made an important decision. I enrolled in a very creative Doctor of Ministry graduate program – The University of Creation Spirituality (recently rechristened Wisdom University) founded by the theologian Matthew Fox. In this intensely experiential program, I further explored my surgical awareness in papers and discussions with peers. Especially helpful were my own artistic depictions of surgery created in "art-as-meditation" classes, revealing the profundity of my trauma and bringing others inside the experience, reducing my isolation. My formal education of spirit, however, was still unfinished, so following graduation, I enrolled in The Chaplaincy Institute in Berkeley, an interfaith seminary, to pursue ordination and a new vision of life.

Not only was there much to learn about religion and interfaith spirituality in this seminary experience, I particularly valued its experiential processes – the ongoing focus on contemplative self-inquiry and vocational discernment. We were constantly applying the world's religious teachings to our own lives and asking questions like, "What is my personal understanding and experience of these truths?" "How am I called to embody them?" "What most deeply expresses the work of my soul now?"

Finally, after three years of study through both graduate programs, ordination felt like an *initiation ritual* for enlightened Elderhood. Standing shoulder-to-shoulder with my fellow ordinands before a huge and loving audience of family, friends, and previously ordained ministers; enveloped by colorful multi-cultural/interfaith music, song, drumming, chanting, prayers, and pageantry; honored by faculty with words that revealed how deeply seen and appreciated I had been; readying myself in awe, wonder, fear, tears, and joy before Divinity as my turn to speak drew close; delivering my sermon as the testament of my soul; being anointed with oil and blessed with a laying on of hands from the entire congregation, and celebrating later with my beloved family, friends, and men's group – I was reborn an Elder, one with clear soul instructions. Specifically, I realized then that understanding aging – its ultimate purpose and meaning – now represented the work of my soul and the new direction of my life.

Transformation

Often, when we speak of transformation, we envision a process of improvement – a perfecting or re-inventing of the self, even its divinization. We want to feel that we are growing, advancing, or bettering our selves. In this conception, however, may lurk the ego's secret desire to be superior, invincible, perhaps even immortal. We may also imagine transformation leading to a blissful state of being, the self transformed in joy. What would happen, however, if real transformation meant watching our familiar self disappear and presiding at its funeral? I had reflected on the idea of self-transcendence in the past, what the Buddhists call "no self," but I did not appreciate how painful and profound this transformation would be.

Following ordination, I returned to my island sanctuary but found, to my dismay, a steadily deepening experience of grief and emptiness. Yes, I had entered a new and amazing time of life, but instead of a journey into happiness and joy, I experienced an even deeper desolation. It filled my chest, surrounded my heart, and suffocated my spirit. I wrestled every morning with intense feelings of grief, despair, confusion, emptiness, even non-existence, falling daily into an underground flow of pain. *I was disappearing*. Like the River Styx separating the living from the dead, this pain created a boundary blocking all roads to the future. Stepping into this flow of pain over and over, deeper and deeper, appeared to be the only way to move forward. On the surface, of course, were happy times – visiting children and grandchildren, interesting writing projects, workshops, new friends, and travel – but the deep pull of loss and grief seemed inescapable. In a way that I could not yet fathom, *I was dying*.

The feeling of death haunted me. It was not only that I felt like I was dying, I discovered (to my horror initially) that I wanted to die. Maybe it was reliving my childhood anesthesia awareness, experiencing my own "death" on the operating table; maybe it was the "death" of my identity, career and community; maybe I was tired of performing, of being "somebody" in the world; or maybe it was all of these factors that created this death wish. Or maybe there was something more. I sensed a yearning to go home, home to God. I realized, then, that not only is death a central concern and symbol in aging, it also expresses a longing (usually unconscious), as if part of us knows its divine purpose and destination. Once I understood and accepted this longing, my horror disappeared and I began to feel more comfortable with the idea of dying and, at the same time, less impatient to "get on with it."

My grief also included the fantasy of family. Somewhere along the line, my children had become independent adults, individuating, now fully launched in their own lives. Transferring their emotional needs to friends, mates, and co-workers, they clearly didn't need me any more, or not like they did once. I missed the old times profoundly – the daily conversations about homework, birthdays, movies, meals, opinions, pets, vacations, dreams, rules, and even problems. Family life! Like so many people overwhelmed in the busyness of the middle years, I had not appreciated how much family meant to me. My wife and I grieved these lost times and often felt lost together. Family now meant visiting far away adult children and grandchildren. Loving and being loved by our grandkids was unbelievably fulfilling, but we always had to leave and come home. These new families were only ours by extension. Most of the time, we were on our own looking for a new life.

I slid back many times into the temptation to search for another identity, imagining a new career, project, or personal story, but, on closer inspection, each new plan, each re-invented identity, lost its appeal and momentum, and disappeared like a desert mirage. Strangely, I just didn't want to "be somebody" any more – whatever that meant, and more deeply, I simply lacked the energy and the will to do so. New goals felt too much like the previous thirty years. Like starting a worn-out model T Ford, I could not crank my old self up again.

Writing about my experiences in this aging process was the only thing that really steadied me. I realized, gradually, that this journey into aging was not necessarily about finding a new identity or occupation, and thus continuing the busy frenzy of the middle years, but about learning to live without such an intense focus on activity, productivity, achievement and purpose. Indeed my energy and will had already deserted me; there was no choice in the matter. This was no longer the pain of my delayed-PTSD; this was an encounter with aging – the experience of an uncertain and seemingly meaningless existence after a lifetime of quest and conquest.

In this expanding vacuum, my well-rehearsed identity and its history evaporated like a puddle on a hot day. My past now played like an old movie, one I was no longer interested in, dream-like, progressively fading away. Old attachments, too, began dissolving – I didn't care so much about the things, places or issues of my past (indeed, I threw away forty years of personal journals without an ounce of regret!). My previous world was gone, had died, but in its place, I started noticing – and exploring – the empty space left by its disappearance.

Then, unexpectedly, in this emptiness, I begin to notice subtle and spontaneous changes in consciousness – expanding moments of silence, stillness, and timelessness, moments when it seemed as if the mystery of eternity was leaking into the everyday world. I was moving into a curious new and peaceful space – *consciousness without thought,* an awareness devoid of purpose, effort, agenda, point of view, or even self. These changes, which had been emerging unappreciated for some time, seemed to increase when observed, and eventually became harbingers of a new kind of consciousness and a new kind of life – intimations of spiritual transformation.

One day it dawned on me: This emptying of consciousness is part of aging! If we enter the state of quiet simplicity and mindfulness potentially available in our late-life experience, that is, if we resist the temptation to continue or recreate all the hectic craziness of the middle years, then self and its various identities, lose their appeal and hold on consciousness, and the whole psychological complex of "me" begins to dissolve. What's left is consciousness itself.

One of my morning spiritual practices all through this period was journal writing, which often involved imaginary dialogues with God. Moving into the experience of Presence, I would share my feelings, concerns and needs with God, ask questions, and await a response that I also wrote down. One morning, to my utter surprise – perhaps shock is better description – the response I received was, *"You do not exist. You are not that person you think you are."* Over and over the words come, *" I am what you are, John. You are me."* In this strange and unfolding dialogue, I confirmed something I had long suspected: that "I" – my identity – was but a fiction, a story accumulated over decades, and that fiction was fading. Left in its wake, however, was consciousness itself and, according to my dialogues with God, that consciousness belonged not to "me" but to Divinity.

Recalling this insight, I am reminded of a spiritual teaching story recently related by a friend. A man dies, goes to Heaven, and knocks on the Heaven's door. A voice answers, "Who is it?" The man replies, "It's me" and gives his name. The voice says, "Go away. There is not enough room for two of us." The man knocks again, is asked once more by the voice to identify himself, repeats his response, and is told a second time, "Go away. There is not enough room for two of us." Finally the man knocks one last time. When asked to identify himself, he says, "It is you." The door opens and he enters Heaven. So it is that we may eventually learn that spiritual transformation requires a realization of who we really are.

Examining my experience in this spontaneously widening consciousness, I also realized that the identity I had developed during childhood and adult years, the basic identity we all form (I am so-and-so and you are so-and-so), had contributed to, perhaps even created, my feelings of loneliness and isolation. If I am this defined and delineated person, then I am separate from you. We can have moments of connection, but we each return to our individual fortresses of personhood, separation and independence. Though my aloneness grew evermore unbearable, I explored it now with renewed courage and determination. I was onto something.

As the angst of loneliness, isolation, and meaninglessness threatened to rip apart my soul, I spontaneously fell into one of two simple practices: shifting awareness back into *consciousness without thought*, which, I discovered to my repeated astonishment, temporarily released the whole painful experience, or focusing consciousness on the all-pervading experience of the divine Presence – known as the "practice of Presence," to feel its unconditional love and safety. Looking back, I realize that these practices both lead to the same unity experience, the former described in more Buddhist language, the latter in more theistic. As the costume of "me" melted away, "I" was becoming something else, something far more amazing and much happier.

This same happiness expanded whenever I dissolved a corresponding inner split. I saw now that my personal identity had also separated me from an inner divine core. The "divided self" had been described for years in the psychological literature, now I understood it from a spiritual perspective. It represented the split between thought and being, between my mentally-constructed identity and the deep experience of the indwelling divine. Focusing consciousness without thought into this dark and powerful center of being felt like stepping into a Jacuzzi of joy, and I recalled the ancient Hindu equation *sat-chit-ananda*, which roughly translates to *existence, consciousness, bliss*. It is all one and I am that – the incomprehensible and ineffable bliss of *being*.

In the outer world, I discovered that I also experienced this same joy of being in two rather surprising places, though looking back, I should not have been surprised. The first occurred while playing with my grandchildren. Roughhousing on the grass, building railroad tracks across the floor, reading endless books, countless hugs, walks in the back yard...I could do these things for hours. Clock, calendar, identity and purpose dissolved in this timeless and spontaneous play. The second place I found this joy was playing my guitar. I spontaneously began to write songs and play music. Words and melodies emerged from the mysterious depths of my own being, and time, again, disappeared in a marvelous unity of sound, movement, and feeling. I saw then how my own goals and beliefs – no matter how compelling – had in fact separating me from the deep joy and spontaneity of just being, and how living in its natural and unplanned flow – found with grandchildren and music, represented one of the most natural gifts of age.

This alchemy of consciousness continued. Without an identity to separate "me" from the "All," I sensed increasingly that consciousness was not in me, I was in it, and it was God's consciousness. And, without the idea of "me" splitting the unity of being, I felt my body to be part of God. In other words, "my" consciousness and being were literally part of the consciousness and being of Divinity. Pretty heady realizations when I tried to explain them, but absolutely natural when I experienced them first hand. My world was shifting on this remarkable axis of consciousness. I was discovering a new kind of man in the process – a spiritual man, whole, full, and free of identity, self, and inner conflict. The more "I" disappeared, the more Divinity filled in.

The majority of these changes in self and consciousness were internal, not big splashy outer events but a subtle unfolding of transformational processes – early springtime buds of enlightenment pushing through the encrusted snow of identity, self and personality. Those around me, including family, did not notice them, but I did, and I followed these changes as a miner tracks specks of gold in a stream. I was discovering that *getting old was enlightenment in slow motion!*

Throughout this experience was the continuing and very real experience of my own physical aging, a process both concrete and progressive. Discussing these experiences with older friends, relatives, and workshop participants brought me face to face with my psychological fears of growing old, fears of illness, incapacitation and dependency, as well as feelings of shame, worthlessness, and helplessness associated with the idea of old age. The more I shared these concerns with others, the more we admitted our anxieties and laughed at our worst-case scenarios, the more we understood and accepted aging as integral to our own humanity, the more these fears receded from consciousness. I also realized that these feelings and issues were related to this fictitious self that was rapidly disappearing. As it dissolved, so too did my fears. As the Buddha might ask, "Who grows old and dies where there is no one there?" Once past this imagined, self-created obstacle, I begin to explore the frontier of aging with growing interest and even excitement. This new dimension of consciousness was changing "me" almost daily.

One of the most awe-inspiring changes fashioned in this white-hot forge of transformation was my capacity to stand in the fire, to respond to the powerful and sometimes overwhelming needs of the moment. I now believe that this capacity signifies the enlightened Elder's readiness to serve.

One February morning, my brother who was vacationing with us, came downstairs after a phone call. Visibly stunned, he says, "Greg is dead." Just like that, an accidental drug overdose stole his oldest son. I drove him the two-hour journey to talk with the police and claim Greg's body. Alone with his son in a drab, depressing mortuary room, my brother talked to his boy, tenderly expressing his love and emerging grief, and finally telephoned his other son and ex-wife to share the experience of Greg's still and lifeless body. I will never forget his sensitivity, gentleness, and clarity during that call. "I am with Greg now. He looks so still and peaceful, as if he were just sleeping. Do you want me to tell him anything for you?" It broke my heart but I stood with him in that room as a silent and loving witness to his loss. I instinctively knew my role in this awful experience was to join by brother's struggle and serve him in every way he needed.

When it looked like my 89-year-old mother's health was failing rapidly, my wife and I moved in with her. Eventually, suspecting a bladder infection, we administered antibiotics and she recovered physically only to begin a long slow decline into dementia. After five months of running my mother's house like a nursing home, our own "caregiver burnout" forced us to place her in an assisted living facility. As she grew ever more confused and disoriented, pleading for help I could not deliver, as her memory failure erased her entire adult life, I could do nothing but be present, supportive, kind, and sad. But I stayed in the fire, visited her regularly and, as power of attorney for healthcare and executor of her estate, wrapped up the myriad details of her life.

My hottest fire, however, was the most inconceivable. I recall it like yesterday: I stood alone at the lectern of the River City Funeral Chapel looking out at the swelling ranks of mourners. Friends, family, and strangers packed the sanctuary and overflow room, and formed a line that snaked out into the parking lot (the director said he stopped counting at 400). The casket stands open and an uncanny radiance lights up the countless flower arrangements spread across the stage. I nodded at the four men awaiting my signal – my men's group of 15 years – and we retreated into the director's office and closed the door. I fell into their arms and wept convulsively for two or three minutes. Then I returned to the crowded chapel, put on my stole, and began a funeral service for my son Adam killed in an automobile accident five anguished days earlier. I met with my men's group again the next evening and cried deeply. One of these men had just finished caring for his younger sister during her terminal struggle with breast cancer, living with her family for three months five hundred miles from his home. Another had lost two brothers and a father to heart attacks in the preceding two years. We were all on the "Road of Trials." We had learned to stand in the fire and to support each other no matter what.

Good times also happened on this road. A minister now, I was blessed with requests to officiate three weddings soon after my ordination. I married my older son, my daughter's best friend, and my oldest friend. These were lovely and loving experiences full of joy. Standing inches away from two people made beautiful in their loving vulnerability, pledging their lives to each other, who are happy and scared but full of hope – is an experience beyond words. I can hear their breathing, feel their nervous excitement, and almost touch the magic of the timeless moment they proclaim their love before a community of family and friends. This, too, was standing in the fire and taking my rightful place as an Elder in the human family. For me, it was the wisdom of age that made each ceremony into a sacred act, where the Heavens open, a living light surrounds us, and the entire gathering becomes one in the miracle of love.

Reflecting on these events, I began to wonder who stands in the fire if the personal self is disappearing? Who cares for his brother's pain, whose heart breaks in the grief of a child's death, who feels the joy of a wedding ceremony? Looking inward, I could see that my responses came from two very different sources. The first source constituted reactions from my residual self that still operated in the human world of everyday emotions. Though it was disappearing, this self could be reactivated amidst the overwhelming drama of major catastrophes. The second source, and the one responsible for my greater capacity to stand in the fire, was the same deep well of being that produced my music and my joy. That dimension of being, I saw, is the divine, and as such, it is both unflappable and one with all being. Dissolved in this center of gravity, I knew without thinking what needed to be done and how to do it.

The transformation of self and consciousness described here took three years to complete. As should be evident by now, it represented a profoundly painful "Dark Night of the Soul," a time when ego, will and self fall paralyzed before something so much larger, a time when suffering and alienation occur in the service of awakening. Though I would not consider myself "enlightened," a word so misused and misunderstood as to be nearly useless, the change in my experience of consciousness and being is miraculous, a transformation that invited me next into a new and divine world.

Revelation

We are accustomed to believing that Heaven exists only in the future, after death, and that you must be "good enough" to get in. The idea that Heaven may also exist in this world, available to all, seems to defy everything we have been taught by religion, culture and common sense. Would you be surprised to learn that teachers from every religion, along with everyday folks who had no religion, have described the existence and experience of Heaven on Earth for centuries?

I grew up without religious instruction. My parents, products of twentieth century modernity, equated religion with super-stition or neurosis and concluded that God was dead. But in early childhood, I needed no religion for Creation surrounded me like a fairyland. The world was fresh and surprising, enchanting at every turn: Earth smells, insect sounds, thunder storms, fall's vibrant colors and winter's cold, crunchy snow. To me, family members were as beautiful and fascinating as gods and my love for them boundless. Most important, the world thrived in an omnipresent magical consciousness, a conscious Presence that brightened the yard with spectral shining radiance. Amidst this wondrously alive and rampant beauty, I lived in Garden consciousness, held lovingly in the timelessness of Divinity. In time, I lost this original wonderland. Exchanging perceptual innocence for the thought-driven world of man, as we all do, I lost paradise somewhere on the road to adulthood.

For much of my adult life I searched the world's religious and spiritual literature for an understanding of my original perception of Creation and a means of seeing it once again. I eventually found what I was looking for in first hand accounts of mystical experiences. In these amazing narratives, everyday folks reported glimpses of "a new heaven and a new earth" all around them – a literal perception of the immanent divine world – and their descriptions perfectly matched my early memories (the literature is full of these accounts but no one seems to have noticed!). My research also revealed that mystics in every religion have said virtually the same thing for centuries: Heaven is found in the experience of the divine Presence, no matter where you are. [1]

I don't remember the first time I re-experienced Heaven on Earth as an adult. Though I had stopped seeing it, I still remembered the joy this omnipresent divine world and had sensed its existence off and on for decades. The truth is that I knew Heaven was here but lacked the courage to say or even believe what I knew. When I finally confirmed my belief, the breakthrough of Heaven on Earth into consciousness wasn't so much an extraordinary event as a simple and intentional amplification of consciousness. Once I understood how to see it, and started looking more intensely, I found it everywhere. Arriving first as an intuition and then as actual perception, I began to see the divine world right before my eyes. Of course! It was so obvious. It's everywhere. We just don't stop to look. But the fullness of this revelation continues to astound me.

The next intuition, however, rocked me back on my heels. As if handed another perfectly obvious conclusion, I realized one day that finding Heaven here held the secret of our new longevity. That's why we are living so much longer! We age not to get sick and die in misery but to progressively transform self and consciousness to rediscover Heaven on Earth. As consciousness empties and sharpens with age, as enlightenment seeps into everyday life, we begin to see the world with a fresh perception, revealing new wonder, beauty, mystery and joy, and inspiring a new reverence for life. The journey of life on Earth ends in old age, but it ends where it began – in the divine world. Everything changes in this new consciousness.

For me, this astonishing realization defines one of the ultimate goals in aging – we are called to awaken the awareness of Heaven on Earth for all humanity, to invite everyone to join us, and, in the process, bring about an entirely new human community. In sum, I believe aging asks us to engage the powerful processes of initiation and transformation *in order to witness and contribute to the building of Heaven on Earth*.

Sensing this implicit "goal" of the aging process is thrilling and constantly motivates me to focus on further "cleansing the doors of perception." Practicing mystical consciousness, *consciousness without thought,* I watch how the intellectual constructs of identity, time and story habitually return to restore the "veil of tears" that obscures my vision of the divine world. I see how thoughts and beliefs function like cloudy lenses distorting perception; how, "lost in thought," I see only what I think, not what is right before my eyes. Again and again, a thousand times over, I rediscover how intensifying thought-free consciousness refreshes the mystical experience of Heaven on Earth. Like elevating the power on a microscope, the beauty of the unseen world returns without fail right before my eyes. For most of my adult life, I lived in the collective stream of negative and fearful thoughts that fill humanity's collective consciousness (it's a "dog-eat-dog" world of ruthless competition, hardship and suffering) and create Hell on Earth. No more.

What is Heaven on Earth like? In a consciousness without thought, sensing the Presence everywhere, my world becomes unbelievably beautiful, saturated with holiness, and infinitely precious. Of course it's the same place, but I witness it in a fresh way – everything washed clean and polished, like springtime in a meadow after a cleansing rain, as if God suddenly sharpened my vision, making every detail of reality incredibly vivid and distinct. My immediate existence is brighter, clearer, more alluring, and absolutely perfect just as it is. Vibrant colors, rich textures, and spell-binding wonders excite my vision. Objects shine with an inner light, translucent with the living consciousness filling the world, rendering everything holy, timeless, and infinitely precious. People glow like angels, their faces radiant. Here there is no ugliness, corruption, or sin, nothing to do or fix, and every apparent "problem" reminds me to stop thinking, remove this filter of negative thought, and return to Heaven on Earth. A tangible loving Presence surrounds and thrills me with joy and I realize anew that God is the substance of all, including me. Each time I "click" back into this intentional mystical experience, burdens, struggles and goals dissolve and I am home again. Each time my perception of Heaven on Earth grows stronger.

As I bring this same thought-free consciousness into my body, sensing that pure energy in the center of my being, I experience a swelling of ecstasy too big to contain. Moved by an eruption of unconditional love for everything around me, I feel like dancing or laughing or just wandering through this magical world. Bursting with joy, I want to engage everybody I see, sharing the love I'm made of. With no artificial limits or mental rules to follow, I feel wonderfully and completely spontaneous, but I restrain my exuberance – I am shy in this child-like wonder. I especially love wandering outside, sensing the energy of Divinity moving through the world, living in everything, appearing in endlessly changing colors, textures, sounds, forms, beings, smells and tastes, all held in a soft and conscious celestial light. I lie down on the Earth, feel her powerful energy and the subtle thrum of life within; touch a tree, feel its consciousness and being; and sense the living space all round me filled with the divine Presence. There is no dearth of wonder in this enchanted land.

Dwelling in the experience of Presence, movement feels effortless and flowing, like that moment in a dance when the music takes over my body and begins to dance me. Swept up in this divine waltz, chores, errands, and jobs become new and fascinating. Playing with children and dogs enchants me the most for they still know and love the magical flow of joyful

41

energy moving between beings. And once in this dance, the idea of "me" becomes so irrelevant it's laughable: the choice between a controlled identity and the freedom of Divinity is a "no-brainer" – no one to be and nothing to accomplish – such delicious freedom.

Conversations pose the greatest challenge me. I resist being drawn back into the world of "problems" and beliefs that make up much of social discourse. I find myself instead being positive, complimentary and friendly, inviting others into the beauty and wonder everywhere. I also resist thinking in this consciousness. As thinking usually hides some kind of mental trap, I ignore or discard most thoughts as quickly as they arise, returning to pure consciousness and the world of the senses. The only thoughts I dwell on long enough to remember are those spontaneous insights that arise from this shift into heightened, thought-free consciousness, insights I want to share with others to bring them into Heaven on Earth. One day I had the paradoxical realization that humanity's search for *meaning* seduces it back into the world of thought and struggle, while pure *sensing* returns everything to the flow of Divinity. Suddenly the phrase "come to your senses!" is strikingly clear.

My life deepens in this consciousness. The angst of loneliness is gone and I grow more peaceful in this inner silence. Because I slide back into habitual patterns of thought, I continue the work of breaking these "chains of illusion" separating Heaven and Earth. I love the progress I am making. Of course everyday life goes on – I pay bills, exercise, see friends, spend time with family, thrill in nature's wonders. I don't proselytize about Heaven on Earth – it's not worth the debate – so I share this world in writing and teaching. Nor do I believe I have to change the world – yet another distressing idea; instead I sense the world is gradually waking up, and that my aging enlightenment is part of that process.

Episodes of atrial fibrillation have recurred and I have now been defibrillated five times (and may choose to undergo a procedure called cardiac ablation). I know that other challenging things will happen in the aging process – illness, decline, dependency and death, and I know that as of this writing, I am still in the youth of old age, before the really hard things happen. Because these thoughts distract me from dissolving into pure consciousness that is my entrance to Heaven on Earth, I gladly release them. I know that my evolving consciousness, and the changes I experience in it, will continue until I die (which is itself another change in consciousness), so I watch, practice, and work on waking up each day in the Garden.

Returning to this mystical consciousness, it becomes increasingly difficult to talk about the Heaven on Earth experience. Ineffable and unbelievable, words cannot hold it and I really just want to melt back into the happiness and love of Garden consciousness. So I end this memoir with words from my ordination sermon describing the ultimate significance of my journey so far.

"For me, this ceremony is not about being ordained for a particular ministry or work but to a mystical consciousness that reveals all life to be Sacred – not as a metaphor but a lived and witnessed reality. Looking back, I realize this has always been my calling, through psychology, writing, spiritual growth, and seminary. It is the calling of the mystic to the sacred...And for me, aging is part of this calling-thread. I am being ordained not to a career but to a time of life with its unique consciousness and tasks... My ordination is about stepping into the divine world so that everything I do now is part of my calling and every action I take is sacred action. Ordination is a baptism sanctifying my life, my aging, and my new role as spiritual Elder. If ordination represents a sacred covenant with Divinity and religious community, then this is mine, and I now step across its threshold."

I am an explorer, wandering in a new dimension of reality, a world with very different conditions and laws from the all-too-familiar world of man. I arrived here, I believe, because the power of initiation released me from the goal-oriented identity and agenda of middle years; because the power of transformation dissolved the veil of thought and self obscuring divine consciousness; and because the power of revelation focused this awakened consciousness on the world as it truly is – Heaven on Earth. This journey was not easy. In fact it was incredibly painful. And it only happened because I was defeated again and again – identity, self and the illusory world all had to cave in. But each time I step into Heaven on Earth, I feel as if I have won the biggest jackpot in the world or walked out the gates of a high-security prison. The truth is, I have – I've won the jackpot of spiritual freedom by escaping the prison of mind, that "hall of mirrors" that keeps us from paradise. I know with absolute certainty that this new perception represents the most accurate and profound experience of reality we can have, one that will someday change humanity.

Part II

The Three Secrets of Aging

Part I told the story of my own still-unfinished aging experience, a life in transition that will in all likelihood continue to evolve as aging reveals ever-new facets and stages of consciousness. In Part II, I want to share with you what I have come to understand about this story so far, that is, the lessons I learned from living through it.

I call these lessons *The Three Secrets of Aging* because they have indeed been well kept secrets. I had never heard of them before. Though I had vague intuitions of what we might find in the land of aging, I was not prepared for the power these secrets held or the road I would have to travel to come to terms with them. Symbolically, my experience feels very much like one of those fairy tales in which the someone's life is cursed by an evil spell, prompting a terrifying journey through darkness and light to find the truth, reverse the spell, and return to the world transformed. Such is the journey of aging.

Part II is intended to help you revision your aging experience, to make sense out of chaos and find deeper value in change. Knowing these secrets ahead of time may not lesson your struggle, but they will provide a meaningful perspective and a goal worth seeking.

Secret I

Aging is an Initiation *into an Extraordinary New Stage of Life*

The events and processes of aging – changing bodies, fading identities, and losses of all shapes and sizes – represent an initiation into an entirely new dimension of life, a time of personal and spiritual growth unprecedented in human history. While aging may represent the end of our old life, it is also the beginning of a new one.

Introduction

Re-living my terrifying experience of anesthesia awareness, I had the feeling that I had undergone some kind of huge and profound *initiation* marking the entrance into a new life stage. I recalled anthropological descriptions of the shaman's initiation and started to see some extraordinary similarities.

Shaman refers to the "physician" or "medicine man" of indigenous peoples around the world, the man or woman responsible for healing the sick through spiritual powers. Becoming a shaman, however, is no easy matter and it's definitely not like going to medical school. The shaman's initiation, typically unexpected and unwanted, invariably involves horrendous physical dismemberment. In an altered state of consciousness, the shaman experiences his body being torn apart by the spirits, subject to all manner of tortures, taken to the land of the dead, and, after all seems hopeless and lost, resurrected. Following this gruesome death-and-rebirth experience, the shaman returns to everyday life with new healing powers from the spirit world and acknowledgement from the community of his potential new function in the tribe.

My adolescent surgical experience was equally horrific – a dramatically altered state of consciousness, bodily invasion, shattering dismemberment, cessation of heartbeat, death-like inert cold, complete paralysis before the god-like agents of my destruction, hands inside my heart, and abandonment to the "land of the dead." No one knew what I had gone through, no one asked about my experience, and no one would have believed it anyway. I awoke feeling murdered and mutilated, and immediately concealed this unbearable horror even from myself – a death hidden inside my psyche ticking like a time bomb.

While my surgical experience was remarkably similar to a shaman's initiation, it was obviously incomplete. First, there was no remembered experience at the time or, to put it differently, no experience of being re-membered – put back together as a new and whole person. I remained divided inside, part of me frozen in psychic death, part of me going on with life. Second, the experience lacked any transcendent significance, that is, recognition of its spiritual potential, power and purpose. Finally, my status or role in the community did not change nor was there any awareness that I had, in fact, been through an initiation. My family was relieved that the surgery was successful and done with, and that was that.

When my adolescent initiation resumed its fierce power four decades later, this time there was meaning. With therapy and review of anesthesia awareness research, I understood what had happened to me psychologically. There was also *remembering* as I relived the trauma and healed my personality. Still missing from this initiation was the realization of new spiritual powers and a new spiritual role in the community (curiously, even though my original surgical initiation was incomplete, I did become a healer, practicing for three decades as a psychologist). With my deeply fulfilling ordination ceremony, however, my shaman-like initiation into aging was finally complete. Affirmed as an Elder, uniquely gifted with sensitivity to divine reality, I embraced my new healing role in the world. For me, delayed PTSD had been medical parlance for the Elder's initiation.

My surgical PTSD also offered a remarkable model of the *death-and-rebirth* transition inherent in the initiation of aging. This symbolic death involved *the complete dismantling of my life* – identity, career, income, community, physical health, and lifestyle, dismembered like the shaman's body. My old life had to "die" for my new one to be born. It is probably safe to say that none of us are prepared for the changes aging will demand of us.

The specific initiatory experiences in the Late Life Passage, of course, can vary widely, sometimes arriving dramatically, like a cancer diagnosis, death of a spouse, heart attack, or retirement, producing a sudden and profound disruption of familiar life; or they may arrive in subtle and gradual ways, like the uncanny and disturbing realization one day that our old life is already gone, that the busy middle years of family and work slipped away when we weren't noticing, leaving only an empty gilded cage. Whether big or small, the initiation hidden in the Late Life Passage should not be underestimated; rather it needs to be recognized, understood, and honored.

Aging and Initiation

With tears in his eyes, Ed, a seventy-year-old man in one of my classes on aging lamented, "All I am is behind me now. How do I live until I die?" With youth, career, and parenthood behind him, death approaching, and no vision of a meaningful present, Ed had lost his bearings. He felt worthless, useless, and forgotten. Worse, like so many seniors, he did not comprehend his suffering as the pathos of an unfinished initiation. The unhappiness of the old – their complaints about aches, pains, and the unfairness of life, their "Why am I still alive?" questions – often disguises this longing to complete aging's initiation into a new life, for they are languishing in the emptiness of the old one.

In the *Midlife Passage*, we surrender our goals of mastery, conquest, and never-ending progress to discover the work of our souls, giving the fall season of life its unique richness and value.

In the *Late Life Passage* of winter, we are asked to surrender the whole project of self, including identity, history, and future in the service of something larger. We need to better understand, then, how aging initiates the Elder and why Elders are so important.

Aging as Incomplete Initiation

For most Elders, the initiation of aging remains tragically incomplete, as suggested by the three most common meanings of the word.

1. In its most general usage, initiation means *to begin something new*. Certainly the process of aging, with its innumerable physical, psychological, social, and spiritual changes, is exactly that – the beginning of something radically new. As none of us have ever personally visited the land of aging before, this developmental passage presents a powerful initiatory threshold.

2. In anthropology, initiation refers to *a cultural ritual* marking and facilitating an individual's transition from childhood to adulthood. Many cultures also have initiation rituals for preparing older people for their new identity and roles as Elders. Sadly, Western Civilization still has no common culturally meaningful rituals or rites of passage for Elders beyond birthday and retirement parties, which tend to be superficial celebrations given the profundity of the passage.

3. Finally, in religious language, the word initiation refers to the *rites, ordeals, instructions, and ceremonies involved in joining a secret society or religious order*. Such initiation vests the individual with special knowledge, duties, and status. Clearly we lack such a society of enlightened Elders in the West – a community of seniors who have been inten-

tionally initiated into the psychological, spiritual, or mystical secrets of aging.

Judging from this etymological analysis, it is evident that our culture's current experience of aging constitutes a profoundly *incomplete* initiation. Though we are surely beginning something new, the personal, social and spiritual significance of aging remains severely underdeveloped and its transformational possibilities tragically lost.

Return of the Enlightened Elder

Native peoples value wise Elders, not only honoring them with special designation and duties, but depending on them in good times and bad for practical guidance, historical knowledge, conflict arbitration, tribal mythology, spiritual awareness, and a living connection to ancestors. In our cultural obsession with youth and the latest technological progress, we have lost the Elder's vision and spiritual consciousness. We look to institutions, science, and technology for the wisdom that should also flow from the truly wise. But something interesting and utterly unprecedented is happening as a result of this very same progress: We are living longer, much longer, and this longevity is creating a vast and untapped supply of *potential* Elders.

For nearly all of recorded history, only one person in ten could hope to live to the age of sixty-five. With the medical advances in the last one hundred years, nearly eighty percent of us in America will live to be past that age, often into our eighty's and ninety's. In the last one hundred years, the percentage of people in the United States sixty-five or older has more than tripled and we have some seventy thousand centenarians now living around us. What was once reserved for a tiny fraction (no wonder elders were honored!) is increasingly available to us all. It's absolutely incredible. But what is this revolution in longevity for? Is it just to grow old?

The Three Secrets of Aging answers this question with a resounding "No." Because Western culture has largely forgotten the Elder's profound and timeless contribution, Elders have forgotten their own destiny. Our aging experience will languish as an incomplete and failed initiation if we do not recognize its potential and respond to its call. In the anguish of boredom, stagnation and insignificance, Elders in the Western world are beginning to search for the meaning of their suffering, pursuing a vital vision quest on aging. The world cries out in desperation for them to find it and return the enlightened Elder's vision, hope and wisdom to the human enterprise.

The Tasks of Aging as Initiation

Every stage of life has its own unique growth tasks. In childhood, we develop our physical, emotional, and intellectual abilities, attach to parents and family, and become social beings. In adolescence we learn about becoming an adult, in areas such as sexuality, love, relationships, responsibility, work, and independence. The conversation now turns to what we need to learn in the initiation of aging.

Succeeding in the work of aging is neither easy nor guaranteed. When events or circumstances alter our lives forever, stealing middle-age values and security, pushing us into an unknown landscape beyond our choosing, we are called to do both psychological and spiritual work, work that transforms loss and change into meaning, wisdom and renewal. I believe this work consists of a set of psychological and spiritual tasks, each task profound in its personal implications. We actually begin working on many of these tasks in the middle years as part of our implicit preparation for aging, but we will work them more deeply and explicitly once the process of initiation begins.

We focus first on the psychological *Tasks of Aging* (listed below), leaving the spiritual and mystical ones for Secrets II and III. To understand how these tasks might apply to your life, read the list as a whole, check the items that stir something inside, and then reflect on the kind of inner work they may be asking of you. Work on these tasks in any way you like – journal writing, meditation, therapy, spiritual direction, or conversations with friends. Repeat this exercise in a few months and you will find new items speaking to you and old ones revealing new insights. Working through these items is not like checking off a "to do" list; rather, consider it a guide to the themes that will sooner or later transform the meaning and purpose of your life. Also, while the items are largely self-explanatory, you are encouraged to delve more deeply into their personal significance by exploring Appendix A.

The Tasks of Aging

Releasing the Identity and Roles of the Middle Years
Discovering the Language and Wisdom of the Aging Body
Learning to Grieve and Survive
Finding the Hidden Meaning and Value of Change
Life Review and Understanding
Growing the Unfinished Self
Finding Meaningful "Work"
Clarifying Religious and Spiritual Beliefs
Opening the Heart
Staying Involved

These tasks certainly characterized my initiation into age. Without releasing my old identity and its roles, I would still be locked into middle-aged values, goals and activities, postponing this journey perhaps indefinitely. Tuning deeply into my body (rather than forcing it to conform to my expectations) helped me learn its new rhythms and trust the changing flow of its energies, which were now moving me like a stream toward a new world. I also had to face and survive my grief in order to explore the hidden meaning and value of these many changes, and to discover how my unfinished self needed to heal before it could be dissolve back into divine being. Meaningful work for me meant understanding the deeper significance of the aging experience – as described in my ordination sermon – and beginning to map out its spiritual dimensions. All this lead naturally to opening the heart and staying involved, for I found a well-spring of love hidden beneath the self and the roles I had played and a tremendous need to express it with family, friends, and other seniors. As you can readily see, this work creates a powerful catalyst for psychological growth.

Like me, you will discover that these Tasks of Aging may take many months or even years. Let the tasks speak to you; let them lead the way. However you proceed, try to be patient with yourself and trust that if you do this work, you will not only come through, you will find new value for your life. This is the work that gives the initiation of age its poignancy and meaning.

Personal Realization of Death – The Final Task.

One day in our aging experience we *know* we will die - not abstractly, not some time in the future, but on a day just like today. Death will come for each of us and there is no escape. For some, like me, this realization arrives suddenly, with the jolt of an earthquake, during a serious illness, accident, or depression. For others, it sneaks up more gradually through the pestering of countless little voices witnessing our changing reflection in the mirror, progressive loss of energy, the aches, pains, and limitations of aging, or the insidious onset of a chronic illness. Facing the reality of personal death constitutes the final and most powerful task in the Elder's initiation.

Though we are loath to admit it, *aging is death in slow motion.* In advancing age, the body begins to retreat, conserving its vitality for the waning years. Eventually arms and legs may feel like tree limbs in winter and youthful passions are but memories.

This unnerving, deeply disturbing shudder of comprehension – that death is our personal destiny, that dying has already begun, that one day our body will actually be dead, and that the majority of our life is now gone - is the reality shock core to the Elder's initiation.

Shakespeare understood this dark insight well. In Sonnet 73, he described it powerfully, and hinted that it occurred in two stages.

Sonnet 73

That time of year thou mayst in me behold
When yellow leaves, or none, or few, do hang
Upon those boughs that shake against the cold,
Bare ruined choirs, where late the sweet birds sang.

In me thou seest the twilight of such day
As after sunset fadeth in the west,
Which by and by black night doth take away,
Death's second self, that seals up all in rest.

In me thou seest the glowing of such fire,
That on the ashes of his youth doth lie,
As the deathbed whereon it must expire,
Consumed with that which it was nourished by.

This thou perceiv'est which makes thy love more strong,
To love that well which thou must leave ere long.

At the heart of this profoundly sensitive appreciation of life's ending, however, is the additional and profound insight that there are, in fact, two deaths in winter: one real, the other symbolic.

We know of our physical death, the one waiting for us at the end, so what is it that dies symbolically in the winter? The answer is the self-idea and its future – this complex construction of identity, time and story progressively dismantled in the Late Life Passage. Eventually the self-idea exists only in memory, which may itself begin to deteriorate. And with the future shrinking as well, we must eventually surrender just about everything that has defined us: parenthood, career, ambition, authority, colleagues, friends, loved ones, hobbies, energy, health, appearance, social standing, cognitive agility, future dreams, even our independence. We watch the life we knew fading like a sunset in the twilight of our day. There comes a time when only a few withered leaves of identity are left hanging on the ego's bare branches, and the person we knew for a lifetime has all but vanished. This fading away of personal identity in the twilight of life represents death's first visit, an experience of unparalleled importance.

It is actually this symbolic personal death that we grieve most deeply in winter. It is here that we say goodbye to the memories, people, and possibilities that comprised our life. All we lived, knew, and loved disappears, and every major loss pulls us down into a grief sometimes too large to bear. Yet this very sorrow is also the work of transformation. If we experience this pain deeply enough, we will discover that it is a necessary, meaningful, and purposeful process. It is the final defeat of the ego.

We experience many losses in the process of initiation. The loss most deeply connected to initiation is often the one, real or symbolic, that forces us to look squarely at our own death. For some, this ultimate realization may percolate inside for months or even years as it does the inner work of ending the *project of me*. Most of us remain in denial, believing that the idea of death is either too depressing, too scary, too far in the future, or, since it cannot be avoided or predicted, better not thought about at all. But denial will only delay or abort our initiation. *Facing our personal death becomes the final task of aging, the one catalyzing our initiation.* It's why revising our wills, making funeral plans, and wrapping up our affairs are such a powerful and transformational exercises. To do its work, the personal realization of death needs to startle, shock, distress or absorb us, even if no one else knows. What comes next will depend on divine providence, for the ego lacks the power or wisdom to initiate itself.

Initiation as Ritual

Completing the initiation of age often includes an actual rite of passage – a formal ceremony marking the movement from our old life to the new one. For me, ordination was just such a ritual recognizing and blessing my new place in the human community. An initiation ceremony can take many forms, from a simple sequence of symbolic actions – a reading, a prayer and a toast completed with a friend, to a complex ritual engaging our larger community. What's important in an initiation ritual is that we feel truly seen, valued, and blessed in the process, honored for who we were in the past and cerebrated for who we are becoming in the future. If you feel the need for formal initiation, discuss it with those closest to you, imagining together the kind of ceremony that would make you feel seen, renewed and reborn. When the imagined ritual feels right, perform it sincerely. The archetype of initiation dwells deep in the soul, like a great underground force, its power larger than we know until enacted. It may become the final step that completes your Late Life Passage.

Gifts of Initiation Passage

The initiation of age, if handled consciously and wisely, creates a developmental transition that moves us from the materialistic concerns of middle age to the awakened consciousness of the Elder in winter. In a gradual but a profound shift, we actually become different, as does our place in the world. For the enlightened Elder - the one who has done the inner work of aging - gifts blossom on the tree of life that have enormous value to self, family, community, and the world. These gifts can be divided into those we receive and those we give others. As before, the name of each gift is largely self-explanatory; further explanations will be found in Appendix B.

Gifts Received

Increased Happiness in a Slower and More Relaxed Life
Confidence in the Ability to Survive Tragedy, Hardship and Loss
Greater Patience, Maturity and Wisdom
Less Concern About What Others' Think
Freedom from Traditional Social Roles and Expectations
New or Revived Interests and Hobbies
Healing and Reorganization of Personality
Psychological and Spiritual Insights about the Meaning of Life
A Deeper Experience of Community
An Easier and Less Conflicted Death

While the gifts received are easy enough to find, what does an enlightened Elder have to give another person? The new gifts we have to give are essentially those of genuine maturity, gifts that have grown from what we mean to others, what we have learned through the seasons of life, and how we ourselves have ripened. As you read the gifts, imagine how each gift might be expressed in your life.

Gifts to Give

Encouragement, Support, and Reassurance
Practical Experience and Ideas
Blessing
Larger Vision of Life
A Personal Understanding of History

Stability
Social Conscience
Unconditional Love
The Ripened Self
Examples of How to Age and Die

Conclusions

Do you see now how important Elders are? We are the stitching that holds life together, the carriers and teachers of meaning and morality, and the mature love through which the young are blessed. As enlightened Elders, we give these gifts as we assume our new roles as parent, grandparent, friend, mentor, family historian, social conscience, volunteer, creative artist, personal example, and crisis manager. We do it wherever we are and simply by the way we are. In the final analysis, we are the gift. The psychological and spiritual work of initiation has been worth the Road of Trials.

Secret II

Aging is a Transformation *of Self and Consciousness*

*Aging is enlightenment in slow motion. It begins spontaneously,
naturally and subtly. As we wake up from the illusions of mind, we
transition from personal identity to the consciousness of Divinity,
giving birth to the enlightened Elder.*

Introduction

In spite of the fact that spiritual interests, activity, and experiences
tend to increase with age, and surveys suggest that religion and
spirituality matter to older people, few Elders describe enlightenment experiences. I believe this reality will soon radically alter.

There are many reasons older people do not report enlightenment, including fear of non-ordinary experiences, limited skill
in discussing spiritual subjects, and lack of exposure to mystical
traditions and processes. But there is another more hopeful possibility. *Perhaps enlightenment begins to happen naturally with
advancing age, but its transformation of consciousness is so gradual,
subtle, unexpected, and subjective that most Elders fail to notice it, and,
as a result, the emergence of divine consciousness goes largely unrecog-
nized and unrealized.*

Based on my own transformations of self and consciousness, I
now view aging as *enlightenment in slow motion,* but we must
recognize and experience this process consciously to awaken its
potential. What if people began to experience age-related
changes in consciousness as essentially *mystical* in nature? What
if they began to trust their own emerging mystical experience, to
allow themselves to discover where it led? What if the subtle and
spontaneous changes in consciousness associated with aging
were actually the beginning of enlightenment and the realization
of Divinity as the truest self?

How might this transformation work? As we move into old age, our familiar identity loses its importance. It is fading or long gone. We also begin to lose interest in thought itself – our thoughts no longer seem so important and seem to disappear more quickly, along with all the underlying ideas that structure our conventional understanding of identity, time, reality, and story. As these contents of consciousness empty, we can become aware of consciousness itself, pure and omnipresent. Exploring this experience, we discover, as the mystics before us, that consciousness is not "mine" but rather part of the vast and all-inclusive consciousness we call Divinity pervading the cosmos. When we experience consciousness directly, free of thought, we are literally experiencing Divinity, and a door to eternity opens in the human psyche. In this unity experience, we begin to notice numerous subtle changes in consciousness.

Subtle Changes in Consciousness in Aging

Subtle changes in consciousness appear spontaneously in the aging experience, preparing the Elder for the progressive unfolding of enlightenment. If we can learn to enter these cracks in everyday awareness, these spaces between thoughts, this transformation of consciousness will quicken and intensify. As consciousness empties of thought structures, we gradually wake up from the thought-created dream of life filling everyday consciousness.

The following list of enlightenment's subtle changes is hardly exhaustive, nor is it necessary to experience each one. Its purpose is to help you pay attention to these spontaneous glimpses of pure consciousness. For example, in your experience of aging, have you noticed...

- A gradual fading of identity, as if who you were or think you are is no longer very important or even that real.

- Relief that you no longer have to "put on" your costume of identity, be somebody important or special in the world, or care about what people think of you.

- A diminishing in the intensity of your emotions, so that you are less controlled or "taken over" by the emotional patterns that used to run your life.

- The progressive dissolution of time's importance in your life, so that clock, day planner, and calendar no longer drive your day, and the distinctions of past, present, and future seem less real or important.

- A loss of "high gear," that hard-driving, goal-oriented focus on getting things done, and a concomitant shift in values from pressured doing to naturally flowing being.

- Memory failures (for names, details, intentions, ideas, and habits) that may initially trigger concerns about senility but instead reflect a letting go of information that is no longer important or meaningful.

- Dropping into a silent and thoughtless consciousness in which there is no purpose, effort, agenda, point of view, or even a thinker.

- Moments of silence, stillness, and timelessness, when it seems as if the mystery of eternity were leaking into your everyday world.

- An awareness of a larger consciousness existing all around you, filling all space and time, and feeling a sense of comfort, peace, and reassurance of its "Presence."

- Loss of interest in and attachment to material things that once seemed important.

- Spontaneous spiritual insights that surprise you with their depth and significance.

- Increasing awareness of the richness of everyday life discovered with a still and empty mind, and an increasing enjoyment of living in the present, sensing every moment as precious just as it is.

- Moments of unexplained and unconditional joy, childlike innocence, and spontaneous playfulness.

- Sensory surprises - the full moon pouring through the window at night, a new blossom on the rose bush by the porch, a child's ruffled hair in the sunshine – that bring awareness of the radiant beauty of the world and provoke feelings of wonder and gratitude.

- A loss of personal boundaries, when it feels as if you are what you're looking at, allowing you to feel one with a tree, a friend, a plant, the Earth, or even the whole Cosmos, and know the world as Self.

- Momentary freedom from the body's habitual self-contraction, that fist-like way we grip our self, producing a wonderful sense of relief, release and relaxation.

- Inexplicable bliss when experiencing the energy of the life force in your body.

- A spontaneous welling up of gratitude, concern and love for the whole world and its peoples, animals, plants, insects, cycles and processes.

Each of these subtle shifts in consciousness represents a seed-moment of mystical consciousness – an awareness of Divinity's consciousness in, around, and through us, dissolving the mind's habitual illusion of identity and separation. We need only to notice, intensify, and assimilate the qualities and effects of each subtle shift in order to accelerate a fuller transformation of consciousness. One way to do this is to turn these glimpses into a spiritual practice.

The *Tasks of Spiritual Transformation* are listed below. Designed to turn aging itself into a spiritual practice, these tasks or practices facilitate the natural emptying of consciousness, amplify the mystical awareness that arises in its place, and prepare us for the ultimate transformation of self. As before, these tasks are not to be done once and checked off the list, but rather explored as continuing experiences to observe and develop. While the tasks are largely self-explanatory, descriptions of each one can be found in Appendix C.

Tasks of Spiritual Transformation

Disbelieving Thought
Experiencing the Consciousness Behind Thought
Seeing Through the Illusion of a Personal Self
Releasing Contraction
Transcending Attachment
Deepening the Experience of Eternal Values
Discovering and Experiencing Mystical Consciousness
Experiencing the World as Self
Finding Intuitive Understanding of Life, Love, and Divinity
Shifting from Performing to Happiness and Unconditional Love

Let's explore the first two tasks to illustrate their use in spiritual transformation. Disbelieving thought means that we begin to question what we think and to notice the effect thoughts have on our feelings and behavior. For example, consider your thoughts about what you should be or do, what's wrong with someone else, or the interpretation you impose on a recent event. How do these thoughts affect you or others? What would happen if you simply dismissed these thoughts? Can you see the freedom that would begin to open up in your life? And what if you shifted your awareness from a particular thought to the consciousness in which it arises? What do you notice when you become consciousness of consciousness itself? Now the fun really begins because consciousness is itself transformative – problem thoughts disappear in pure consciousness, and in pure consciousness you start to discover your original nature. Moving down the list in this way will bring you countless surprises and amazing new ways of living.

Each time you notice one of the Subtle Changes in Consciousness, or explore one of the Tasks of Aging as Spiritual Practice, take a moment to heighten your awareness of it. Step into the change and see what else you discover, how the experience deepens, and what happens next. Noticing these changes can stimulate a progressive chemistry of mystical awakening, but we have to work on this change over and over until it takes. If we accept that aging is meant to be a mystical experience, our motivation for transformation will quicken.

The Problem of Self Re-Interpreted

The birth of the self-idea – the idea of me – helped humans became *self-conscious*, a remarkable evolutionary step which in turn created the spiritual potential for knowing the Divine Self, our inborn divine nature. Unfortunately, this experience of consciousness was quickly hijacked by the false self – the belief in a separate, independent, mortal, and endangered person –

which spread like a virus leading to the "ills" of narcissism, greed, competition, and violence.

The Divine Self consists of pure consciousness and being. Like energy and matter, or the wave and particle nature of light, consciousness and being are actually one, though we generally lack the ability to experience this unity directly. The self-idea, or false self, created and maintained by a dense construction thought, has enshrouded the Divine Self for most of recent human history. When the self-idea disappears, however, divine consciousness begins to fill and reorganize the personality in ways that transcend the ego's limited vision. Consciousness, in turn, transforms the experience of our own physical being into the divine being. Only the greatest religious teachers, saints, prophets and poets realized this mystical fusion of consciousness and being as the Divine Self. In sum, the self-concept has long been a case of mistaken identity.

Although never connecting it to aging, mystical Christianity understood this transformation well, suggesting that Divinity arises within us when the personal self and its story dissolve. The Eastern Orthodox Church calls this transformation "theosis," or union with God, which is said to result in the individual's deification. The mystical branches of many other religions such as Hinduism, Buddhism, and Islam similarly recount in poetry, song, and scripture how dying to the small self allows the larger Self to fill consciousness with its vast and loving Presence. From this larger consciousness, we experience a new life in winter and become, in effect, a bodhisattva, the Buddhist term for an enlightened being who remains in the world of problems in order to serve the spiritual growth of others. So it is that the enlightened Elder lives increasingly in, and from Divinity's consciousness and being to love and serve the world.

Keep in mind that this change in consciousness, rather than being sudden, complete, or perfect, usually arises slowly, gradually, naturally, appearing off-and-on, and may not even be recognized at first. Nor is this new awareness anything heroic - we are not waking up to personally save the planet, yet another story allowing ego to hijack consciousness. Instead, Divinity's consciousness and being are experienced in and as "my" consciousness and being. From this experience, we discover the gifts that flow from enlightened consciousness, and share them with our part of the world, touching friends, spouse, grand-children, neighbors, pets, plants, parks, church, and all the details of everyday living. In this way, we are each called to be conduits of divine love exactly where we are.

What Becoming the Divine Self Is and Is Not

Given the endless misconceptions we have in this culture about what enlightenment really means, I want to provide some additional clarification on what this transformation of consciousness is, and is not, to ensure we really understand what we're doing.

Divinity is what exists, as pure consciousness and being, before thoughts, concepts, and beliefs create a separate false self. Divinity is the consciousness of your consciousness, the being of your being, the presence of your presence, and the self of your self. You are experiencing God right now though you may be too distracted, busy, or disbelieving to notice. But becoming God is not what you *think* for there is no thinking, or at least not in the conventional sense. Instead, becoming God opens into a consciousness and being beyond thought. Whatever is discovered in that consciousness can best be described as revelation.

This transformation of self does not mean that "I" alone am God, for that would represent colossal egotism and misunder-standing; rather when the self-idea, its story, and associated emotional states, are released from awareness, what is left is God. In other words, "I" do not become God for "I" (the ego and its false self identifications) must disappear in order for the Divine Self to fill in the empty space. As a result, there can be no self-inflation for there is no false self to inflate. The expectation that *I* will become all powerful or all knowing is simply the ego's grandiose fantasy.

Everyday Living without a Personal Self

How do you live without a personal self? Life actually goes on quite easily, far more easily in fact than when the false self dominates consciousness. Thoughts, feelings, conversations, and actions still take place, there just isn't a separate false self to get entangled with them.

Complex behavior devoid of an inner thinker or director is in fact quite common. In activities as diverse as creativity, lovemaking, skiing, yard work, house cleaning, or cooking, the thinker/director often disappears altogether for extended periods. Your original nature has no form, purpose, or plan other than to be as it is in the moment, and it is to that original divine consciousness and being that you return again and again. The true self is Divinity flowering, flowing and awakening a whole new experience of freedom, generosity, love, mystery, joy, wonder, and holiness. Experiencing our divine consciousness and being heals wounds, dissolves conflicts, and returns the sacred to everyday living. Indeed, the split between sacred and secular disappears, and soon only God exists.

There is, however, the *problem of vacillation*. In mystical consciousness, life is a timeless flow of being and becoming bubbling with wonder, happiness and love; then suddenly, an old worry, contraction, or addiction clicks back in restoring the familiar world of problems and reactivity. This recoil can happen subtly as thoughts sneak back in to steal consciousness, or powerfully in the wake of unexpected upsets, but either way the experience of consciousness and being is forgotten and all the familiar ego-driven story and its illusions absorb us again.

Whenever vacillation occurs, spiritual practice is essential. The false self and its point of view will always disbelieve and discount what we see, know, and experience in mystical consciousness. Vacillation challenges us to avoid listening to the ego's self-idea and familiar fears. As we resist debating with the false self and step back into mystical consciousness, we return to our divine self that instinctively knows the way of unconditional happiness and love.

Mystical Consciousness

For me, the most valuable gift of Secret II is the continuing flowering of mystical consciousness: Divinity's consciousness experienced in, through, and around me as the very essence of my "own" consciousness, transforming my experience of being into divine being as a vessel of joyous energy and activity. Without the structure and boundaries of my former professional identity to create a distracting persona, the ability to experience mystical consciousness is still expanding. I seek it again and again for direction, comfort, inspiration and wisdom. Over and over, opening to divine consciousness and being dispels doubts and reassures me that this ongoing process of transformation, no matter how "strange" it might seem to others, is the unfolding truth of my Late Life Passage.

The Gifts of Transformation

A new variety of gifts emerges naturally and spontaneously from the thought-free, timeless, and joyous subjectivity of mystical consciousness. Noticing and amplifying these gifts contributes to their growth and expression. As before, the gifts are self-explanatory (descriptions can be found in Appendix D), and they are again divided into those the Elder receives and those available to give.

Gifts Received

The gifts born of mystical consciousness for the Elder are truly miraculous. They include the following experiences:

Gifts Received

Comfort
Silence of Mind
Freedom in Flow
Peace
Waking Up
Self as World
A New Center of Consciousness
Wisdom and Ultimate Knowledge
Sheer Joy

Gifts to Give

Gifts to give mature later than those received because they must first ripen in the Elder's transformed consciousness before flowing on to others. These gifts include.

Gifts to Give

Unconditional Love
Compassion
Increased Capacity for Direct Contact
New Teachings
New Psychic Capacities

The unfolding of these gifts takes time. We don't suddenly rush out into the world as an enlightened Elder. Each must learn to note and integrate these new spiritual potentials in natural and skillful ways. The more you notice the gifts listed above, the more often you will find them hidden in your own experience. Try to discover how this ocean of divine consciousness includes and moves you and be sure that the old you doesn't try take over by imposing its familiar style, goals and attachments. Stay in mystical consciousness and you will observe an evolution of your involvement in the world happening on its own. Then the final gifts both received and given will blossom from the new roles you play in the world. Of course, there is really no "you" to play these roles, but the roles exist nonetheless, for they serve as funnels for the mystical consciousness of Divinity to flow into Creation.

One Man's Spiritual Experience of the Initiation of Aging

An 80-year-old man recently shared this description of a spontaneous Elder initiation experienced somewhat later in aging. The catalyst was an illness. The spiritual consequences were surprising, especially to him. Bob explained,

> *I came on my old age suddenly and I'm not sure what spirituality is. I had pain in my back; I could barely walk; I had surgery, became infected and spent 2 1/2 months in rehab. When I returned home I discovered that, really for the first time, I was old. And that discovery turned my religiosity and then my spirituality around. While I was in the hospital, I had a dream where something I identified as God told me to return to church—my drug induced conversion. I had become skeptical of my life-long practice in the Catholic Church almost twenty years before and had stopped practicing.*
>
> *But when I was able, I returned to the Church (it was what I knew) although never with the wholehearted belief I once had. I attended and continue to, but only as a means of focusing my thoughts on the something beyond me, a something which I don't understand at all. When I was younger, I thought that religion, belief and beyond that spirituality, had to be founded on rationality. I came out of schools teaching Thomas Aquinas and Scholastic*

philosophy; in fact, I really gloried in that rationality. Not so anymore. It doesn't bother me now that I don't understand what I believe. And that I possess a much more restricted set of beliefs. And the beliefs don't include doctrines. I have taken the Beliefnet survey a couple of times to see how my beliefs would be seen by an outside source: the first time I was identified as holding the beliefs of a Quaker and the second as a Unitarian. Buddhism was in the top 3 both times. Church is now a place that offers a community and a relatively common morality, and I divorce it from the institution.

In a sense my world has narrowed: my concerns are now close to me—family, friends, community, and a world I don't seem to be able to make much of an impression on. I pray, not that someone somewhere is going to make something happen, but that I can be at peace with what has and will happen and perhaps play a part in making good things happen. The prayer often brings me peace, but not from an outside agent.

I have often heard that, as one ages, old beliefs, rules, patterns become rigid. That's not what's happened to me. I certainly hold some rules and values strongly, but none so strongly that I would risk hurting someone to hold to them. All actions occur in a context, and that context must always be considered.

In the past, I have been something of an isolate: I was friendly but had few friends. I still have few friends, but I value them tremendously and wish I had more. The men's group meets a real need for me and is treasured. I feel the need to let them know how much they are valued and are my friends. Perhaps that's a result of my sense of my impending demise, but it really seems important

I don't know if this has anything to do with spirituality, but these are important elements of my life now. I'm not much interested in an afterlife, because there is so much here to be experienced and acted upon.

I've enjoyed thinking about this, even if I haven't offered any help.

In this man's eloquent and humble reflections, we see how profoundly Bob was affected by his Late Life Passage of illness and hospitalization, and how former religious beliefs softened into spiritual intuitions, and these in turn evolved into subtle mystical experiences of closeness or unity with the divine. It has been a gradual change, one he might not have fully noticed had he not written these reflections. The result has been a far simpler life devoted more naturally to loving others and being at peace. His words sweetly illustrate most of the gifts listed above. Has he fully transformed the self? No, but he could and he is still changing. Bob just needs to understand the transformation already taking place and then amplify it further by focusing on his own direct experience of divine consciousness and being.

Conclusions

Enlightenment represents a profound intensification and purification of consciousness. As consciousness empties of the thought structures comprising duality, Divinity is found to be our true and original self, expanding our capacity for unconditional love, generosity, appreciation, wisdom, and joy. Aging as spiritual practice creates an opportunity for divine consciousness to blossom through our own transformed and clarified consciousness, and for Divinity's being to animate and energize our own being. Then, one day, we realize that enlightenment was always nearby obscured only by our "problems," which consist primarily of distressing and erroneous thoughts. In the silence of mind, we find out who we really are. Such joy.

Secret III

Aging is the Revelation *of Heaven on Earth*

*As the veil of thought dissolves in conscious aging, Heaven on Earth
begins to shine everywhere and the world is sacred once again. We
have come home from our long journey through the world of thought
and invite others to join us in a new consciousness of Creation.*

Introduction

Having traveled this far with me, you are ready now for the third
and final Secret of Aging: In Divinity's awakened consciousness,
ordinary reality – this place, this time, this situation – is transfigured into a world of extraordinary beauty, wonder, and
perfection. More than that, it becomes holy, for the mystics from
every tradition tell us that reality is Divinity in substance and
form. Gradually, or suddenly, we discover that our transformed
consciousness now reveals the radiance of the divine world
everywhere. So what's the secret? Wake up! Heaven on Earth
shines all around you.

Heaven on Earth

The world's mystics have described Heaven on Earth for
centuries. That this holy experience constitutes the greatest gift of
aging, however, is a new idea. Perhaps few elderly people have
experienced sufficient enlightenment to notice this divinely
radiant world. Maybe our cultural prejudice, equating aging with
suffering, forbids the old to realize or speak of this revelation
(we're supposed to be miserable in old age, right?). I suspect,
however, that many Elders have seen Heaven on Earth and
simply come to rest in the divine world without really understanding it, or if they do, without needing to name or explain it.
Whatever the reason, Heaven on Earth awaits us, sparkling like

diamonds in the divine perception of transformed consciousness.

Heaven on Earth goes by many names in the world's religions – the Pure Land, the Garden of Shiva, the Kingdom of God – but it's all the same place: the ordinary everyday world transformed and transfigured by awakened consciousness. Consider the declarations of these world-famous teachers (read them only if you need convincing, if not, if you already sense this reality, go on to the next section): Jesus, Christianity's founder, proclaimed: *"The father's kingdom is spread out upon the earth and people do not see it...What you look for has come, but you do not know it."*[2]. Ramana Maharshi, the famous Hindu sage added, *"This is the Kingdom of Heaven. The realized being sees this as the Kingdom of Heaven whereas the others see it as 'this world.'"*[3] Thich Nhat Hanh, the beloved Buddhist monk, told us, *"You don't have to die in order to enter the Kingdom of God. It is better to do it now when you are fully alive...The Kingdom doesn't have to come and you do not have to go to it. It is already here...There is not one day that I do not walk in the Kingdom of God."*[4] In his book titled *Heaven on Earth*, Rabbi Faitel Levin concluded, *"The ultimate communion with G-d" takes place here...in relating to G-d as found in the physical itself – This world is not an antechamber: it is the palace itself."* [5] Al-'Arabi, the great Muslim scholar, taught that the perfectly realized man also witnesses the divine *"...in the heaven of this world"* [6] and Sufi poet Firdausi exclaimed, *"If on earth there be a paradise of bliss, it is this, it is this, it is this."* [7] Li Po, a Chinese Taoist poet, confided, *"If you were to ask me why I dwell among green mountains, I should laugh silently; my soul is serene...There is another heaven and earth beyond the world of men."* [8] Finally, Native American Chief Seattle put it this way: *"Every part of this earth is sacred to my people. Every hillside, every valley, every clearing and wood, is holy in the memory and experience of my people."* [9]

So how do we make sense of these astonishing claims? Eckhart Tolle explained, *"A 'new heaven' is the emergence of a trans-formed state of human consciousness."* [10] That's an important clue.

What is this consciousness? Over 100 years ago, Richard Bucke called it "Cosmic Consciousness" and said the person experiencing it *"is lifted out of his old self and lives rather in heaven than upon the old earth – more correctly the old earth becomes heaven."* [11] New Thought writer, Joel Goldsmith, clarified, *"Heaven and earth are not two places; heaven and earth are one and the same: Earth is our mortal concept of heaven, and heaven is our real awareness of the earth. In other words, heaven is earth correctly understood."* [12] Joseph Campbell, the renowned scholar of religion and mythology, eloquently summed up, *"This is it. This is Eden. When you see the kingdom spread upon the earth, the old way of living in the world is annihilated. That is the end of the world. The end of the world is not an event to come, it is an event of psychological transformation, of visionary transformation. You see not the world of solid things but a world of radiance."* [13] But Benedictine author Joan Chittister may have said it best, *"Am I 'going to heaven'? No, I am already there and it is getting more heavenly every day."* [14]

These sentiments perfectly match my experience of aging. As consciousness cleared of thought and self-preoccupation, as I moved from *conceiving* my environment with thought to *perceiving* it in sensory wonder, the world became ever more magical. I felt as if I had been released from the stranglehold of my old self, and in the process, released from my old world as well. Heaven has become my real and direct awareness of Earth now, for the veil of thought and belief no longer obscure it. This psychological transformation marked the end of my old way of living in the world and it does get more heavenly every day.

Some would argue that Heaven on Earth cannot possibly exist in the midst of the cruelty, suffering and evil witnessed in the world, and this argument is one of the greatest obstacles to realizing the third secret. Just because people do terrible things to one another does not negate Heaven's existence here, it simply means perpetuators of violence and hate are tragically blind to its presence. They live in a self-generated emotional hell. More importantly, the moment you defend this argument you exchange the direct perception of Heaven on Earth for skepticism and disbelief. Rather than argue about suffering and evil, experience the divine world for yourself. Only then will you see situations and events differently.

If Heaven Is Already Here, Why Don't We See it?

Heaven is not somewhere else, not just in the next world, and not only if we are good enough. We are already there, now. So why don't we see it? There are several reasons:

First of all, we do see it, but we don't realize what we are seeing. We tend to experience Heaven on Earth when we are in love; incredibly happy; when wonderful things happen; in the midst of heightened natural beauty, like a sunset or waterfall; during the runner's "high" when endorphins alter consciousness to a state of near euphoria; or during spontaneous mystical experiences. Does this list jog your memory? You've seen Heaven on Earth countless times whenever consciousness expanded naturally into the immanent divine. Abraham Maslow, the father of humanistic psychology, called these moments of altered consciousness "peak experiences" and found that, with guidance, nearly everyone could remember them. Sadly, we often dismiss these Heavenly glimpses, telling ourselves that it was "just" a beautiful day or temporary high. Why?

For most of our lives, we're trapped in a mental thought-world. Instead of seeing Heaven on Earth, we see what we think. As human beings developed their amazing capacity for thought, we fell in love with ideas, creating a virtual second world in the mind, and stopped witnessing the divine world right before our eyes. Over twenty-five hundred years ago, Buddha observed, *"We are what we think. Everything we are arises with our thoughts. With our thoughts we make the world."*[15] In this thought world, we experience only our concepts, beliefs, stereotypes and prejudices: a run-down building, an old man, an irritating family member, a chair or table, a frustrating job, an alcoholic. These concepts filter our experience so completely that we stop witnessing what is right before us. Worse, we're not supposed to see it. The prevailing mindset in this culture is that life is dangerous and we have been expelled from the Garden. Instead of Heaven on Earth, we see scarcity, competition, hardship, struggle, and danger. All the pain, fear and conflict that dominate our world arise from this mindset.

The final reason we fail to see Heaven on Earth is that we are simply too busy to stop and see where we are. Living in a state of chronic fear and frenzy, who takes the time to "wake up and smell the roses?" Not only are we unaware of the possibility of Heaven on Earth, we never look. But the enlightened Elder, the one who understands the first two secrets of aging, understands that this table, that book, this building, this moment – shine with the infinite beauty and divine radiance of Heaven on Earth.

We find Heaven on Earth because it is here, because we have unknowingly longed for it all our lives, and because the consciousness of Heaven on Earth answers all our prayers and the world's greatest problems. Having known (but forgotten) the magic and joy of the divine world in early childhood, we unconsciously long to return, to find the hidden gate to the secret garden and come home again. All we need is knowledge and a key – the knowledge of Heaven's presence here and now and the key of mystical consciousness to unlock the gate of awareness. Heaven on Earth would not be present unless we were meant to find it. *Heaven on Earth is the new world awaiting humanity and the Elder's job is to reveal it.*

In the heightened, thought-free consciousness of awakened aging, the informed, willing and enlightened Elder will find Heaven on Earth everywhere, as beautiful and perfect as the first day of Creation. We discover in this new world an increased appreciation for the everyday life, an ability to see the world through the eyes of our grandchildren, and an enjoyment of the simplest pleasures discovered in the aging experience (fresh fruit, a good sleep, a friend's touch, the smell of wet leaves in the fall). This achievement seems huge only because it is so foreign to us - who even talks about Heaven on Earth as the Elder's destiny? For the enlightened Elder, however, Heaven on Earth illuminates the world like a light bulb in a Tiffany lamp illuminates its colored glass, the most obvious thing in the world. If the enlightened Elder symbolizes our potential maturity, then Heaven on Earth represents our potential destiny.

How Does the Enlightened Elder Find Heaven on Earth?

The transformational power of the first two secrets sets the stage. In Secret 1, completing the Tasks of Initiation releases the past, freeing the Elder for a completely new stage – and experience – of life. In Secret 2, silencing thought in pure consciousness removes the beliefs and concepts that veiled the Divine World, opening the perceptual gates for Secret 3, the realization of Heaven on Earth. The Secrets of Aging have been leading us here all along.

Natural changes associated with aging, in combination with the Elder's awakening consciousness, stir this new perceptual capacity. Below is a list of the natural changes that "cleanse the doors of perception," preparing the Elder for this final revelation. These very same changes can also become the basis of a spiritual practice amplifying their intensity in preparation for the ultimate revelation. As before, the name of each change is largely self-explanatory; further descriptions may be found in Appendix E.

Preparing for Revelation

Quieting the Mind's Inner Chatter
Living a Slower and More Conscious Life
Surrendering Our Obsessive Future Orientation
Appreciating the Present As It Is
Living in the Presence

Changing Our Ideas of Reality

The beliefs that make up the world of thought, that distance, objectify and explain everything, cause us to view the world as if it were something other than Divinity. It takes only a handful of enlightened ideas to shift our whole understanding and perception of reality. To restore our innate capacity for sacred vision, we need only reframe our everyday experience in mystical language and then experience it. Here is a short list of the concepts that can transform your seeing; explanations can be found in Appendix F.

Changing Our Ideas of Reality

The world is not what you think.
This is the divine world.
The universe is conscious and alive.
You are made of God.
Only Divinity exists, everything else is an illusion.
Life is a revelation not a problem to be solved.
Now is all there is.
Enlightenment is happening right now

Practice these vision changers. With a clear and open mind, contemplate each phrase. Sense its message, meaning and implications. Let these simple ideas change the way you see the world.

Gifts of Revelation

A cornucopia of gifts pours forth from the revelation of Heaven on Earth. Once again they may take the form of gifts received and gifts to give and a full description may be found in Appendix G. While this bounty is literally infinite, perhaps the most important gifts, which we both receive and then give back, are these:

Gifts from Heaven on Earth

Beauty
Love
Joy
Freedom
Community

Aging and Death in Heaven on Earth

In the way of all created things, our bodies go on aging, even in the wonder of Heaven on Earth, continuing our life-long human metamorphosis eventually ending in death. Whether this process fills us with gratitude, anticipation and joy, or engenders the fear, anger or regret of the personal self fighting for survival, depends on our level of awakening. Yes, parts of us will sag, break down, or become ill; accidents may happen; we may grow weak and dependent; some will die before us and then our turn will come. Either way, we pass into the mystery of Divinity from which, long ago, we imagined ourselves separate. The key word here is *imagined*, because, in fact, we never left; beliefs in identity, time and story tricked consciousness into the illusion of a separate individuality. In dying, this personal illusion and its apparent physical incarnation dissolve.

As such, dying offers us another spiritual practice. It asks us once again to release the contraction of the fearful self, still clinging to its personal survival, into the all-permeating, all-loving consciousness of Divinity. In the process, we dissolve steadily into the unfathomable, ineffable and formless realm of love and unity. This shift transcends words and must be known directly to transform us, though we have experienced it in lesser degree many times – in falling asleep, making love, and self-forgetting ecstasy. Surrendering to the divine in this same way illuminates the path of conscious dying. Tears will come, losses will be felt, and yet, just beyond the grief, all will meet and surrender into the divine mystery as butter melting in a warm pan.

As teachers from across religious traditions have suggested, what happens after death depends on our state of consciousness at the end and how attached we may be to our familiar self-image. With consciousness habitually merged with the imagined self, most of us will continue in our customary form on the other side (though Near Death Experiencers tell us we will be younger and healthier), where we will meet loved ones who went before. After the journey of individuality moves through various states and places of mind, we may seek another form in this world or another to learn more about the joys, struggles and lessons of ego and incarnation. If, on the other hand, self and identity have already melted into the unitive center of being, we may instead elect to disappear entirely and become the One who loves and projects this entire dance. Either way, we follow the path of our progressive awakening.

Conclusions

Endless and endlessly replenished, the revelation of Heaven on Earth will completely change life as we know it. We have been heading here since the dawn of time. Now we begin, here is where it happens, and we will all be part of the new dance. Tune in, turn on, but don't drop out. Stay and play instead. All of us belong to Creation and together we will see and build "a new Heaven and new Earth." Like Peter Pan urging the audience to save Tinker Bell's life by believing in magic, we must join together and believe in the magic of Heaven on Earth to save ours.

I appreciate that many will still find the Heaven on Earth to be an inconceivable and perhaps even ridiculous idea despite my best efforts to describe and explain it. In fact, this secret may be the most difficult one to unwrap, for it dwells on the further reaches of humanity's evolution of consciousness. Still, this is what I have found and it is too universal a realization to be mine alone. I share it with you in the hope that you will be inspired to search as I did and to one day discover Heaven on Earth for yourself. I have come home. You can, too.

Part III

A Spiritual Blueprint for the Enlightened Elder in the Twenty-First Century

Introduction

We live in a time of unprecedented and nearly cataclysmal change. Our institutions – law, banking, government, science, medicine, religion, education, and family – barely handle the colliding forces now shaking the world. Nor can conventional problem-solving paradigms anticipate or deal with the toxic mix of faltering economies, nuclear proliferation, radical regimes, terrorism, poverty, drug abuse, the still-unfolding drama of climate change, and years of reckless chemical pollution that now threatens the very the web of life. Meanwhile the global internet and social networking technology build a geometrically-expanding web of communications fast approaching a crescendo when billions of people will directly contribute to humanity's cultural and political evolution on a daily, even hourly, basis. But to what end? At the brink, amidst accelerating social change, this period of human history spreads confusion and new knowledge, chaos and new order, unfamiliarity and reconnection. Everyday we seem to wake up in a new world.

History understands this unraveling of conventional reality – that dualistic thought-world we still live in most of the time, as part of a recurring cycle. Whenever civilization embraces superficial values, growing rigid, corrupt, unjust, profane, and uninspiring, the social order descends toward anarchy and darkness. Yet eventually this descent also releases humankind's innate hunger for mystical awakening as the ultimate source of new purpose and values. The greatest teachers of the Axial Age – Buddha, Lao Tzu, Confucius, Moses, Jesus, and Muhammad all stepped forth during periods of enormous cultural turmoil, immorality and dissipation. Because this present time of change is so radical, the specific characteristics of our emerging future defy prediction. But they will necessitate a new way of being in the world. Specifically, I believe a shift from conventional to sacred reality is underway, one that will fulfill the implicit prophecies of enlightened teachers everywhere. And Elders can hold the frame and show the way.

Becoming an Elder at the dawn of the twenty-first century poses incredible challenges, opportunities, and responsibilities. Despite myriad uncertainties, I believe the following divinely-inspired evolutionary innovations will inform this new era:

The End of Business As Usual

America's social character has long emphasized an extraverted, action-oriented, warrior disposition, accompanied by an insatiable drive for conquest and consumption, and periodic orgies of greed and self-inflation. In three short centuries, this orientation swept across the lands, peoples, and creatures of this vast continent, crushing or assimilating everything in its wake, and producing inconceivably violent military weaponry. Destructive and unsustainable, this way of life is ending.

A Return to Our Senses

Humankind emerged from an Earth-based mystical consciousness still evident in many indigenous peoples. This consciousness experiences the Earth and all her beings as sacred, equal, and part of the divine milieu. With the intellectual, social, scientific, industrial, and technological advances of civilization, we progressively separated ourselves from this original spiritual communion with nature, presuming instead that the world solely existed for our use, exploitation and consumption. As the Earth's ecosystems teeter toward a frightening disequilibria of climatic and political forces, we must discover a deep Creation-centered harmony based on sensing the divine world every-where.

We will solve our problems by sensing the living consciousness of the Earth, right here, right now. Coming to our senses means experiencing the Earth directly as a vast, intel-ligent, living and divine being everywhere expressed in a marvelous diversity of forms and processes. Ironically, science embodies this urgent shift to sensation (albeit without a mystical orientation), prizing careful and direct observation over self-serving beliefs. It should come as no surprise that science interrupted our short-sighted narcissistic consumerism with the catastrophic news of global warming.

With a return to our senses, we immediately witness the costs of the warrior archetype – ravaged forests, polluted waterways, failing ecosystems, dying species, and starving peoples. Celebrating the profound gifts of sensation, rather than consumption, would allow the Earth to heal, grow, and renew. More importantly, we will recognize that we *are* the Earth and cannot survive if she dies. In this Earth-revering consciousness, we re-awaken in the Garden. Everywhere I go I see bright, industrious, motivated people reinventing everything they do to serve this global transformation of values and consciousness. In the consciousness of Heaven on Earth, a new kind of civilization is born.

Full Inclusion

The return to Garden consciousness must include all creatures and life forms. In the sensing mode, we quickly discover that sentient beings constantly communicate with each other and with us, we need only learn their language in place of imposing our own. As we learn to listen, the plants and animals of Earth will teach us so much more about her systems, processes, and cycles. Like indigenous peoples, we will recover a life in harmony with our brothers and sisters in this sacred Garden.

Recognizing the infinite value and capacity of each and every individual in creating a new world, we welcome all who wish to help. Everyone has something to offer, and with all the work that needs to be done, there should be no unemployment in Heaven on Earth. Whoever you are, you are invited to participate in giving birth each day to this new Creation and to tend it as the Garden it is.

Decentralized, Local, Participatory Leadership

The time of the patriarchy, with its rigid, hierarchical, centralized, top-down leadership, is also ending. It served its historical purpose of organizing large and complex human systems, but alone cannot solve the problems of the world. The new human organization will likely consist of countless overlapping local, regional, and national circles, each fulfilling a designated function, all relating to one another through other circles, and none "higher" or "lower," more or less powerful, than another. No longer will we place some people above others in power and authority, limiting problem-solving to the few and losing the talent and wisdom of the many. Each of us holds a piece of the puzzle.

Our institutions, ossified in so many ways, need to be reinvented *from the bottom up*, especially education, government, healthcare, business, and religion, so they might become more welcoming, exciting, creative, flexible, local, open, and truly productive. This will take great courage and inspiration, but we all know how to listen, love, cooperate, and create. The talent is here; we lack only the will, and we must find it or perish. At present we fall back on written laws to manage conflict because we choose not to trust and respect one another. When love replaces fear, our laws will make much more sense.

Letting Go of Isolated Personal Security for Intentional Community

For us Elders, one of the most important circles of participatory leadership is found in the creation of intentional community. Financial independence, even when it exists, does not fill the day-to-day void of social isolation and meaninglessness in the Elder's world. Nor do retirement facilities run like country clubs, hotels, and hospitals, understand our deeper needs for creative control and authentic relationships. Grandchildren, too, as precious as they are to us, will grow up and be on their way, and adult children, beginning to anticipate taking responsibility for our lives, sometimes feel more directive then helpful. What we need most in this new time are other Elders. Who else knows what we are going through, what we value now, and what we fear most?

One of the best places for an Elder to find his vision and voice may be small, self-organizing mentoring groups. Drawing older people who feel either a deep frustration with their lives or a deep yearning for more meaningful engagement with others or the world, mentoring group members would commit to meeting regularly for months in order to assist each member in exploring the meaning and purpose of life, work through the tasks associated with each secret, and identify and dissolve obstacles to new creative expression. Providing inspiration, encouragement, and reinforcement, such small mentoring groups hold the potential to awaken and activate Elders in ways never before conceived.

Building on mentoring group experiences, enlightened Elders also have the potential for creating small, self-selected and self-governing senior communities focused on shared values and resources, committed and loving relationships, and activities that encourage personal and spiritual growth, creativity, healthy exercise, play, and meaningful work in the world. Elders in such communities may retain their own homes or move into various forms of co-housing that meet their emotional, financial, and medical needs. In fact, social networking groups are already bringing Elders together in interdependent ways, sharing skills, resources, and caring. The goal of such communities is to reinvent aging and build, from the ground up, the psychological and spiritual home we are each implicitly seeking. The circle of intentional community would, of course, overlap with other circles (for example, family, church, creative enterprises, volunteer work, political action) but maintain its primacy in the Elder's life.

An Urgent Call for the Enlightened Elder

Facing this new world of accelerated global and local change in conventional reality, our importance as awakened Elders is greater than ever. In a time of shifting values, traditions, structures, and goals, our wisdom – and enlightenment! – are critically needed to manage such chaotic social evolution. Enlightened Elders – those of us who have found initiation, transformation, and revelation in the journey of conscious aging – are needed to step into the void everywhere. Through volunteering, care-taking, mentoring, creating, teaching, activism, praying, or socially-conscious business, enlightened Elders have so much to offer. Focused on giving not taking, our common mission is to apply clear vision, well-earned life skills, enlightened perception, and deep wisdom right where we are. The world can't wait for someone else!

The Mystic's Way

While we are born with a mystical nature, our cultural pendulum has swung too far toward reductive materialism and now fails to encourage this divinely-given gift. Our direct sensory perception of Divinity as Creation, on the other hand, restores our original path that I call *The Mystic's Way*.

The Mystic's Way is not reserved just for saints, prophets and gurus. We can all become mystics, especially Elders who have understood the *Three Secrets of Aging*. This new path, virtually a new evolutionary process, is grounded in the following processes, experiences and revelations arising in the context of conscious aging:

- *Mystical consciousness*, that is, a heightened, thought-free awareness of the immanent divine consciousness pervading all existence.

- *The divine self* comprising the recognition that personal consciousness and being are already one with Divinity's consciousness and being, and trusting this unity experience as a source of meaning and action.

- *Progressive transformation* of self and consciousness described by the great mystics in every tradition whose words still illuminate the way for the rest of us.

- *Deep ecumenism* – embracing the highest mystical teachings from all the great religions and wisdom traditions – as our common heritage and birthright.

- Spontaneous and *unconditional love* for the world inspiring confrontation with all forms of duality, dishonesty, and desecration.

- *Service* in which all are called to be mystics, prophets, teachers, saints, artists, priests, and bodhisattvas to embody Divinity in human enterprise.

- *Collective human evolution* as we find and share the divine milieu with one another.

- *Spiritual fulfillment* as we realize that everything we ever wanted – and so much more – is already here.

The Great Work

Visionaries of our time, including Teilhard de Chardin[16], Brian Swimme and Thomas Berry[17], and Matthew Fox[18], describe this collective human enterprise as the "Great Work." The Earth, they say, is a living system differentiating within its own field of spirituality and we are an indivisible part of its evolutionary unfolding. The story of this amazing unfolding, now told through the theories and discoveries science, offers an amazing new cosmology of the sacred, a myth common to the entire human family.

At the individual level, the Great Work arises from the depths of our own being where we are one with and moved by the universe, by Divinity, in its sacred cosmogenesis. *The Three Secrets of Aging* provides motivated Elders with inspired guidance on The Mystics Way into the Great Work.

Secret 1, Aging as an Initiation into a New Stage of Life, asks us to willingly, graciously, and even gratefully, release the past, who we were and all we have, and step across the threshold into a new life. Will you do this?

Secret 2, Aging as a Transformation of Self and Consciousness, asks us to transcend our habitual, thought-driven identity and way of life, awaken mystical consciousness, and discover action born of union with Divinity. Will you do this?

Secret 3, the Revelation of Heaven on Earth, asks us to witness Divinity giving birth to the divine world moment-by-moment and take part in the unfolding the Great Work. Will you do this?

How Do You Find Your Part in the Great Work?

This time of transition holds the promise of a new kind of humanity. Each of us will contribute a unique and critical piece to the whole. If you need further guidance in finding your part, consider these suggestions:

- Go back over the sections that envision personal change (the Tasks of Aging, Tasks of Spiritual Transformation, Preparing for Revelation, and Changing Your Ideas of Reality) and see where your current work is. Go deep into these transformational experiences.

- Explore the gifts found in each secret and pursue the ones holding the most energy or excitement for you. How might you unwrap and offer your gifts?

- Revive your capacity to play, have fun, and create, for these, too, are divine gifts meant for the building of Heaven on Earth.

- Reconnect to the innocence of the "inner child." A young child, still undivided, knows Heaven on Earth directly. When we feel, release and enjoy our inner child, we energize the Divine Self to work and play in the world.

What is the Final Blueprint for the Enlightened Elder?

It's you!

It's wherever you are!

It's whatever these secrets show you!

You have been sensing your place in the world all through this book, surrendering the outworn, transforming consciousness, and seeing anew. Now, with new eyes, see who and where you really are, and begin to do what you love most.

That's your place.

That's your blueprint.

You are the enlightened Elder.

As the kids say, just do it!

Psssst – It ain't over yet!

Appendices

Appendix A. The Tasks of Aging

1. **Releasing the Identity and Roles of the Middle Years**. We often hang onto the identity and roles of the middle years too long. After all, we accomplished so much and felt so important! For men in particular, leaving work triggers an unexpected shock – the "retirement crisis." Suddenly, identity, status, job-related friendships, productivity, life satisfaction, and earned income all disappear. Some researchers argue that this trauma is rare, citing negative findings from large-scale survey data.[19] When questioned more deeply, however, 95% of men report moderate to severe difficulty adjusting to retirement, a finding underscored in interviews with their wives.[20]

   Women, too, face grief and disorientation with the end of gainful employment, though perhaps less intensely given the tendency to play multiple caretaking roles. Still surrendering occupational status and attachments can merge with other age-related losses, including mothering responsibilities and culturally-defined physical attractiveness, to stir feelings of emptiness, self-doubt, and sadness. Not surprisingly, many delay this crisis consciously or unconsciously by postponing retirement or transferring our lifelong work ethic to hobbies, volunteer work, or part-time jobs.

   Another aspect of releasing the identity and roles of the middle years involves letting go of our adult children. Just as we needed to emancipate from our parents in young adulthood, our children need to emancipate from us. They may love and cherish us, but now they need their own friends and their own family more. This is individuation not rejection, but it's important that we don't impose guilt or blame about their shift to independence no matter how hard it may be for us. Our job is to create a new life with our own friends and community. Yes, visit at holidays, shower the grandchildren with love, be available to your children with wise council when asked, but let them go on their own path now.

2. **Discovering the Language and Wisdom of Our Aging Bodies**. While most of us resist tuning into our aging body, it is nonetheless a guide of unparalleled importance. Physical decline, illness, accidents, pain and other symptoms, pull us into the life of the body, which can become a wise teacher. Ask your body how it feels, what it needs, and how your activities affect its quality of life. Are you pushing yourself too hard? Do you experience stress-related physical symptoms? Are you being compassionate with your physical self? Given an imaginary voice, the body will speak its mind.

    One of the most common changes that come with an aging body is the lessening of energy. Because we run out of energy faster (and eventually lose the "higher gears" altogether), we need to determine what's really important and what's not. Spending time with grandchildren or friends may be much more meaningful now than cleaning house. When we can't do both without collapsing, choose the activity that matters most. Changing or lowering your standards is adaptive intelligence not failure. The body's changing energy and consciousness will reveal the most natural way to live now, and one day, the natural way to die. The body already knows how! Remember, too, that research consistently affirms that exercise is medicine for mind, body, and spirit, just don't overdo!

3. **Learning to Grieve and Survive.** There is no avoiding grief in the aging process. Losing cherished dreams, old friends, family members, good health, even the family home – sometimes the pain can seem unbearable. Grief is the work of facing these losses and accepting the feelings that come with them. It is the emotional work of healing, one memory, one heart-sorrow, and one cry at a time.

    Do not be afraid to grieve. Grief is not the enemy, no matter how much it hurts. Rather, grief tells us how much we loved one another, how deep our connection was, how profoundly the person touched our life. When we grieve, we are opening the heart to the truth of love. And grieving slowly heals – releasing our pain, increasing our sensitivity to others, and keeping our loved one in our thoughts and feelings. But we have to realize that grief will not break through just once, we will grieve again and again with every memory, every birthday, every anniversary, and every telephone call that doesn't come, and each time can feel as intense as the first. In this way, like a purifying fire, grief transforms us and slowly we find our own way of accepting and living with our great loss. We will never stop missing the person or circum-stance we lost, but one day the loss will not be so painful. Simply surviving our suffering, however, can be a victory of enormous significance, one that eventually opens a space that will fill with new life. Whenever grief calls, try to feel it, but be sure to take it in reasonable doses and be good to yourself in between. In grief, we learn how to feel, survive, and renew.

    Another grief-filled job of aging is to help our parents die. This may sound harsh or insensitive, but it presents a fundamental responsibility and a loving service. Dying can be difficult and scary. We are there for our parents in their final months, weeks, or hours so they will not die afraid and alone. Our parents also need to finish the business of their lives and heal old relationship wounds, often with us. Be sensitive to their needs. This is the final chance to say "I love you" in word and action.

A final aspect of grieving is confronting physical decline and dependency. As independence diminishes through the stages of aging, we need repeatedly to face feelings of helplessness, incapacitation, and despair. Each step requires us to let go, grieve, adapt, regroup, and go forward in new ways. We also need to accept and prepare for the possibility of more serious illness and incapacitation at the end of life's long journey – stroke, heart failure, dementia, cancer – and the truth is we have to die of something. Knowing that people will be there to listen and care, knowing that we will have the necessary support, and preparing to accept how the end will come for us – these are the ways we turn fear and dread into preparation, planning, prayer, and acceptance.

4. **Finding the Hidden Meaning and Value of Change**. Change often holds hidden yet profound lessons and opportunities. A serious illness may yield time to reflect on our life in uninterrupted or deeper ways; sitting with a dying friend may provide a chance to feel and say things never before expressed; the unexpected catastrophes of others can bring opportunities to serve them; personal crises encourage us to overcome our pride and learn to ask for help. Finding such hidden meaning does not imply that we deny our anger or distress about change, but rather that we search for its additional unseen value, increasingly evident in the light of our psychological and spiritual growth through the preceding years.

5. **Life Review and Understanding.** What has my life been about? What happened to me? How did it turn out? What have I learned? Revisiting the many lives we have lived in this single journey, telling our story to others, writing a journal or memoir, digging deep for insight and understanding, such inner searching opens the door to personal wisdom. Honestly recounting the major chapters of our life, we discover their hidden meaning and significance, especially those parts that seemed most difficult, painful, or still shrouded in shame, guilt or embarrassment. So much will begin to makes sense from the perspective of time and age. Go deep and compost all that life has given. Many discover that releasing old identities and slowing down opens old wounds, wounds that were masked or compensated for by the accomplishments, routines, friendships, security, and self-esteem provided in the workplace. These wounds return in subtle ways at first – vague states of anxiety, melancholy, or rumination. Listening perceptively to the feelings underlying these states will gradually reveal the original wounding circumstances – childhood experiences of loss, rejection, humiliation, or failure that need to be sensitively processed to resolve. In this working through process, we realize how much our work identity and goals seemed to "fix" our wounds, until now. We don't have to rework all our wounds, just the ones that invite us back.

    Life review also entails healing and releasing the wounds of the middle years. We cannot successfully move through the Late Life Passage still entangled in mistakes and problems created by our adult behavior, decisions, and relationship struggles. Whatever regrets, failures, wounds, or guilt we still carry concerning family, friends, and co-workers need to be faced, grieved, healed, and surrendered. In the process, we seek to atone for any harm we have done by asking forgiveness or making amends. On the positive side, releasing the middle years also means recognizing and celebrating our achievements – which we certainly deserve to do – and then letting them go so we can be free to grow anew.

At a larger level, forgiving and releasing the past means reconciling with our personal fate. Everyone on Earth has a personal fate: We grew up in a certain historical period with its unique circumstances, problems, advantages, and challenges. A variety of specific physical, familial, economic, and cultural circumstances produced the experiences that shaped our life and made it different from the lives of others. Aging asks that we reconcile with this fate *because it is ours*. Otherwise we may resist, hate, or bemoan our life, and remain imprisoned by the past. In the end, we need to accept whatever happened even if we didn't particularly like or choose it, make it our own, and discover how it served our psychological and spiritual growth.

As we understand and heal our own unique life, we recognize the larger forces that shaped our journey as inevitable, invaluable and universal. Growing up, falling in love, learning to work, caring for family, losing loved ones, getting old and dying – all this is what makes a complete life. We recognize that no one does it perfectly and that love and work comprise its most important ingredients. This kind of wisdom not only serves as an antidote to suffering, it also stirs an appreciation for the collective human experience, widening our capacity for love, compassion, and gratitude.

Looking back brings up yet another facet to our life's journey - purpose. Embodied in our unique psychological temperament, deepest nature, and compelling interests, a unique sense of purpose can often be found running through our life, like the thread connecting everything we have felt and done. Understanding this purpose can yield amazing insight into the meaning of our life as a quest or search. Aging research further suggests that this sense of purpose is connected to greater feelings of well-being, less fear of death, and a longer life, even in the most dire circumstances[21]

Finally we need to revisit our parents' deaths. The inevitable destination of aging is death, and the deaths that teach us most about this experience are often our parents', buried deep in the psyche like an unvisited grave. The way our parents died may feel like our own fate, but it need not be. Our work is to understand these losses and discover their personal meaning so we don't automatically assume ours will be similar. This process allows us to heal and accept the way things were, discover what we want our dying to be like, and understand what our children may need to learn from our final journey.

6. **Growing My Unfinished Self.** What have you always wanted to do or be? Is it about learning to love, having fun, gardening, being confident, speaking Spanish, or ballroom dancing? Personal growth means expressing these interests – parts of our unfinished self – that we never had time for. It also means trusting the unconscious. Every night, wisdom from the unconscious generates the symbols, images, and stories of dreams. Every day, spontaneous fantasies, slips of the tongue, unusual intuitions and impulsive actions reveal buried needs, emotions, and insights. Get in touch with these expressions of the deeper self that normally stay hidden, for they hold the key to growth. Our growth is not finished in winter; it just needs psychological gardening.

Then let life grow naturally, without trying to control or dominate it, otherwise your "new" life will simply repeat the old one.

The biggest obstacle to spontaneous growth and meaningful work in the later years is rigidity. Trapped in lifelong habits, years go by and nothing changes. To further awaken our capacity for real growth, we can begin to explore new forms of creativity (art, poetry, crafts, hobbies, games, drama, music, dance) and tie them to our deepest values. Creativity has the potential of turning old people into new, not only figuratively, but literally in the stimulation of cellular growth in the brain, new patterns of thinking and feeling in the psyche, and new physical activities for the body. Novelty is the key, interest is the motivation, and joy is the result.

7. **Finding Meaningful "Work" at Every Stage.** Closely connected to purpose, personal growth, and creativity is meaningful work. If we understand work to be the motivating expression of our true self – who we really are inside, then we never lose our need and will to work. At various times, our work might entail spending time with a troubled family member or friend, exploring our genealogy, cleaning out overly-stuffed closets, making new friends, working in the yard, volunteering for a valued cause, starting a spirituality book club – the possibilities are endless. Keep in mind, too, that meaningful work keeps evolving, so we need to re-examine our goals whenever life events provide new directions or boredom signals the stagnation of past goals.

8. **Clarifying Your Religious and Spiritual Beliefs.** What are my religious and spiritual beliefs about God, ultimate reality, the meaning of life, and what happens at death

and beyond? Can I spell them out in enough detail to see if they feel right? Do they bring me comfort or anxiety? Do I need to talk to someone about my feelings and beliefs (a religious professional, psychotherapist, spiritual director) or spend more time in prayerful contact with the divine?

Deepening our beliefs may also ask us to spend more time in silence and solitude – time alone for quiet, reflection, and review. Indeed, many of these tasks require this kind of positive spiritual aloneness. In the silence, we listen inwardly for inspiration and direction, and often a new voice is heard or intuited, our own! It comes from a deeper and wiser place inside, a more mature and realized self that has been waiting all our life to be heard. As we listen, our religious and spiritual beliefs will grow clearer and more meaningful.

Belief, of course, matures in the experience of Divinity, becoming trust and faith. If we sincerely wish to let the divine into our lives, we must learn to trust life, however it happens, even when we cannot understand the purpose. At the highest level of faith, all that happens is Divinity even if we fail to discern the spiritual meaning of events. And, as the ego loses its power in the twilight of life, it must wisely learn to trust that which it returns to.

9. **Opening the Heart.** We already know how to love. We have loved over and over again in our lives – family, friends, lovers, pets, jobs, beauty, music, and sunsets. We can choose to expand this loving to all we encounter. Not every minute, not in every situation, but increasingly we can extend this ability to love unconditionally and unselfishly to all. A vital capacity often hidden for decades behind our proper or ambitious outer persona, opening the heart to one self and the world spreads joy

and compassion everywhere. It is perhaps the greatest accomplishment of aging.

10. **Staying Involved.** Opening the heart also means staying involved. However our lives change, life asks us to continue caring for the world as friend, lover, mentor, grandparent, volunteer, activist, gardener, community member, nurse, or guide. Sometimes it means taking a stand for – or against – something in the service of justice and love. And in doing so, we find out that the world is so much more precious and beautiful than we ever realized.

Staying involved also means maintaining old friends and making new ones. Social support from family and friends is a critical ingredient of positive aging, and isolation is the enemy. Everything gets worse when we are isolated, increasing the risks of depression, substance abuse, and dementia. Friends bring new perspectives on problems, stimulation for growth, and the comradely and humor that make everyday life worth living.

Staying involved continues to be important even in advanced age, when our life empties of possessions, family, friends, places and activities. One day our world may be a single room visited by a handful of family and old friends. In this process, however, we can still stay involved with those around us, including roommates, caregivers, plants and animals. We never lose our need to care. Indeed this need keeps us human, brings us meaning, love and gratitude, and even extends our life.

Appendix B. Gifts of Initiation

Gifts Received. Enlightened Elders describe many gifts received from the aging process, including:

1. **Increased Happiness in a Slower and More Relaxed Life.** A recent survey of 340,000 Americans found that people over 50 feel less worried, stressed and angry.[22] As we surrender the cultural rules, responsibilities, ambitions, and high-paced performance of the middle years, we slow down and relax into a life of greater happiness and ease, living increasingly in the natural rhythms of the body and psyche rather than the driven productivity of the workplace.

2. **Confidence in the Ability to Survive Tragedy, Hardship and Loss.** While doubts about survival swirl in the midst of tragedy and loss, surviving to discover the possibility of a new and meaningful life stimulates a tremendous growth in confidence. We may not be fully healed, we may not like how things turned out, but we faced the worst and we're still here. More than that, we learned profound lessons from the experience and found important and inspiring reasons to go on. Our increased confidence is deserved and we can share it with others through their hardest times.

3. **Greater Patience, Maturity and Wisdom.** Survival also teaches us that overcoming hardships usually takes longer than anticipated. Only patience helps, and a determination to get up everyday and keep going, and the love of a family and friends. Patience, determination, and love – these are surely critical ingredients of maturity. Once we have passed this threshold, we understand that many

problems are not so much fixed as survived, and that healing – the emotional capacity to find meaning, hope, and new goals – is as important as any imagined cure. After facing the same issue, situation, personal flaw or problem over and over, we finally know how to deal with it. We cease useless behavior, let go of pride or the need to be right, and find that life often solves our problems on its own. Our wisdom has been well earned.

4. **Less Concern About What Others' Think**. With maturity comes a wonderful and liberating disregard for what others think of us. For example, surviving the indignities of hospitalization, replete with the absence of privacy, boundaries, and self-determination, or the defeat of losing our home and moving in with family or to a "retirement" facility, or the embarrassment of emotional breakdowns – these experiences can take us far beyond worrying about what others might think. Caring little now for the opinions, judgments, and gossip about us, especially from strangers, adds to a growing sense of independence.

5. **Freedom from Traditional Social Roles and Expectations**. Surviving hardship and loss, and caring less what others think, also reduces our concern about performing social roles properly. This is our life and we will do with it as we please! Freed from the implicit rules of proper social behavior, particularly those superficial relationships that often characterize middle age, we are free to choose the kinds of friends and relationships we truly value or to spend time as we like, including time alone which can provide the wonderfully healing medicine of solitude, quiet, and reflection.

6. **New or Revived Interests and Hobbies**. Life naturally begins to thrive again with the inspirational return of old interests or the development of new ones. We want to learn again, make new connections with others, or discover ways to express important feelings and values. Perhaps we start to plan a memorial or foundation to continue the work of a loved one. Perhaps we spend more time with grandchildren, who now buoy us up with their natural energy, intensity and love. Maybe we find time to unpack an old creativity that in turn brings us back to the life of artistic expression. Whatever form it takes, this re-awakened creativity energizes the soul, stimulating new dreams, possibilities, and activities that bring us back into life.

7. **Healing and Reorganization of Personality**. Facing the reality of personal death can stimulate a fundamental reorganization of the personality. We realize that continuing to live a life devoted to the false self would be a tragic mistake and that ambition will never meet our deeper human needs for love, contact and inclusion. As the self-project crumbles, however, and as we see and grieve our foolishness, the heart begins to open to the needs of the true self denied for so long. What a relief not to have to be "important" or "successful" or "good;" instead we can learn to feel and befriend our basic human nature and, from it, build a new and healthier kind of life.

8. **Psychological and Spiritual Insights about the Meaning of Life**. With increasing life experience, we begin to intuit the larger meaning of life – why things happened the way they did and what life is really all about. As we apply these insights to our lives and to the lives of others, a whole new perspective opens up. Now we understand so

much more about the seasons and cycles of life, what suffering is about, where Divinity fits in, and how to live with increasing authenticity and love. Expressed in alchemical symbolism, meaning transmutes the *prima material* of life's events and processes into the gold of insight and wisdom. Some of the insights are psychological, reflecting a deeper understanding of the needs, motives, and conflicts that influence behavior, ours and others'; and some are spiritual, reflecting larger metaphysical forces shaping our lives. Ultimate meanings arise naturally when we reflect on life, providing a sense of intrinsic purpose and value.

9. **A Deeper Experience of Community**. After years of relating to others in social and work settings, we've grown to understand how important authentic community really is. Not the false community of identities, hierarchy, popularity and power, but a real community of loving souls committed to each other and to personal growth. Increasingly we seek to belong not only to our own family, but to the human family and the family of all living things. Security and love, we realize, are not found in power of possessions but in people.

10. **An Easier and Less Conflicted Death**. Having made peace with so much in our life, understood and forgiven our self and others, healed old wounds, and in the process earned a much larger understanding of life, death takes its rightful place as the natural conclusion to the profound experience of living. Completing our work here, we can let go of life with less regret and conflict, recognizing that death is not our enemy but instead yet another sacred transformation.

New Gifts to Give

1. **Encouragement, Support, and Reassurance.** The young come to Elders with their problems. They come to us because they get discouraged. The gift of encouragement, support, and reassurance says to them: "You can make it. You can overcome these problems. Keep trying, I believe in you." We, too, received this gift growing up. Do you remember how important it was?

2. **Practical Experience and Ideas.** When an Elder helps a younger person from their own field of expertise or competence, a lifetime of practical experience is being offered – knowledge of the "how to's", the pitfalls, and joys of the field. Just as importantly, Elders also share their failures, which gives the younger person permission to fail and to learn from failure - for we certainly did. As we share our experience with a younger person, we support and witness how they blossom.

3. **Blessing.** Often when a younger person comes to an older person, they have chosen that person for a specific but usually unconscious reason. They sense in the Elder's life or achievements something that is inside them as well, but they do not know how to get at it. They are implicitly saying, "I see your gift. I see it because it's in me, too. But I'm afraid to believe I could ever by like you." So, whether it's auto mechanics, carpentry, working with people, or music, our role is to bless the younger person's gift by seeing, naming, and encouraging it, and by acknowledging that the younger person is just where we were once.

4. **Larger Vision of Life.** Having personally lived through numerous problems, crises, historical eras, and cycles of

life, the Elder embodies a larger vision of how things work. An Elder can see, for example, how a certain marriage or career cannot succeed yet must persist as a medium for the individual's personal growth. Although it is not always wise or possible to intervene, our job is to understand the larger task the younger person has unconsciously chosen and hold that person in our heart. And when advice is sought, the Elder is subtle, supportive, and patient, reminding the younger person that problems are how we grow and that life is a learning experience. Often our job involves helping the other work through their problem rather than providing them the solutions.

5. **A Personal Understanding of History.** Elders carry the larger history of family and culture for the young. For example, Elders hold the family stories: "Who was Aunt Tillie?" "When did great grampa leave Russia?" "Why did you and dad divorce?" And they carry memories of earlier times - world wars, depressions, droughts, moon landings, and how people lived before indoor plumbing, supermarkets, color TV, computers, and cell phones. In this way, Elders carry the continuity of human experience through their own lifetime. By telling our stories, generations are brought together and family myths created that will hold and inspire generations to follow. We talk about our own life, for it is theirs as well.

6. **Stability.** Elders provide stability for family and community simply by showing up and taking their places. But I'm talking about mature Elders, people who know how to participate in life, not simply people who are old. An interesting example of this kind of stability was often seen in the men's gatherings that took place

during the 1990's as part of the men's movement. In these all-male conferences, older men were often asked to sit up front and face the audience. Being honored as Elders was not only wonderful for them, for few had ever received such acknowledgment, but it also stabilized the community. The younger men sensed the mature presence of Elders and began to look to them for guidance, leadership, wisdom, and fathering. Because the older men did not seek this status, there was no hidden, political, or self-serving agenda; rather they were simply grateful to serve. This partnership of older and younger men held the gathering in a natural stability that is sadly lacking in our culture today.

Another interesting, hopeful and age-validating gift of the Elder's stability is reflected in the recent discovery that countries with older populations are more peaceful. Demographers tell us that countries with "youth bulges" (more than 40 percent of the population between the ages of 15 and 20) demonstrate two and a half times the internal conflict than others.[23] As the percentage of the population in the second half of life increases, the appetite for war declines. As we have seen, age proffers greater calm and reason, another gift of our growing longevity. In these and other ways, Elders provide an invaluable source of peace and stability amidst the conflicts, sorrows and catastrophes of the world.

7. **Social Conscience.** Beyond self-centered motives and with a voice filled with experience and maturity, the mature Elder can often speak as a social conscience - confronting injustice, neglect, cruelty, warfare, and greed in ways that command attention. An articulate Elder says to the family or culture, "Stop! You are better than that. Face the truth!" A voice of moral rather than institutional

authority, it comes from a place of profound and humbling experience with life's journey, trials and revelations. We stand up for what is right in the world with a new and self-less vision.

8. **Unconditional Love.** More in touch with core human needs, motivated now with empathy and forgiveness, and their own spirituality, initiated Elders are more accepting and kind to others. In the mature Elder's psyche, all these qualities meld into unconditional love. The world needs this kind of love everywhere, and any place it exists is changed. Elders are the voice of unconditional love in the world and love to express it.

9. **The Ripened Self.** The emotional self ripens in the winter of life, particularly when we have learned to accept, trust, and support it. This self fills with a deep and pure nature, shines with its own spiritual presence, and is grounded in wisdom of years. We've all known older people who seem to radiate goodness, kindness, creativity and love. Simply being around this kind of person is a gift. That person also dwells in each of us and will appear when given a chance to blossom. Ultimately, the self is our own divine being.

10. **Examples of How to Age and Die.** Do you remember how your parents and grandparents completed their lives, and the lessons taught by their examples? Whether we know it or not, Elders are living examples of how to age and die. Though we may feel ignored and neglected, we are being watched carefully - videotaped by the minds of the young. Elders are the most important personal examples the young will have, the ones they will draw on when their winter comes. So at the end of

life, let your self be fully human: vulnerable, dependent, receptive, loving, scared, forgiving, needy, and grateful. And let others help. It is our last gift to them.

Appendix C. The Tasks of Spiritual Transformation

1. **Disbelieving Thought.** Although thought and reality are never the same, we often believe our thoughts are true representations of the world, that they accurately reflect reality. With age and experience, we begin to see how deceptive thought can be, and how competing interpretations of reality lead to rigidity, conflict and even war. We are not what we think nor is the world. From a spiritual or metaphysical perspective, thought has been a great deceiver. As we age, we also have less need for complicated beliefs; rather, simple direct experience, appreciated without explanation, dogma or argument, brings us closer to the beauty, perfection and ultimate nature of existence itself. As we transcend thought, we find freedom from the "known."

2. **Experiencing the Consciousness Behind Thought.** As thought loses its hold on us, we can become consciousness of consciousness itself, and in the process, discover that it is everywhere, pervading everything. In fact, consciousness – vast, pure, timeless, empty and omnipresent, is found to be our essential nature, uniting us with the consciousness of Divinity. With the power to transform the experience of all it touches, consciousness is the Holy Grail, the philosopher's stone, the alchemical process that brings enlightenment.

3. **Seeing Through the Illusion of a Personal Self.** As we release thought, so we surrender and dissolve the personal self, for it has been a mental construction all along. We have been constantly spinning fantasies about the idea of "me," fantasies to direct our behavior, manage our image, and try to control the outcome of events.

When this illusion is released, all the associated problems go with it. Who can have personal problems when no one is there? Increasingly we discover the joy and freedom of "no self."

4. **Releasing Contraction.** Emotional life in the thought world inevitably reflects fear and control – fear of bad things happening and attempts to control outcomes so they don't happen. In this control process, we physically "grip" our inner being tightly like a fist, tensing every muscle, forcing it to do what we believe has to be done. We can, on the other hand, choose to release this whole contraction process. We know when this release has been successful when our breathing deepens and expands, as if we can finally take a full and relaxed inhalation and fully let it go. In that moment, we are completely and truly free.

5. **Transcending Attachment.** As identity, plans, abilities, and even people disappear in the emptying of aging, and as we grieve each one, we begin to learn the lesson of non-attachment. Attachment creates suffering, Buddha said, and in our excessive valuing of material and worldly things, we become prisoners of ambition, acquisition, and dependency. We similarly attach to thoughts, fantasies and beliefs. Non-attachment, alternatively, awakens a profound sense of freedom from these constraints and the ability surrender to the natural flow of life.

6. **Deepening the Experience of Eternal Values.** Living in the rich simplicity of thought-free consciousness in the present moment naturally deepens the awareness of the eternal values, values like beauty, simplicity, quiet, love, forgiveness, humor, friendship, generosity, nature, eternity, and God. In the process we become more like the

values themselves - simple, quiet, loving, and beautiful - for we are being transformed by our ongoing experience of divine consciousness.

7. **Discovering and Experiencing Mystical Consciousness.** Awareness of spontaneous changes in awareness leads naturally to the skill of mystical consciousness – an awareness that is intensely-focused, thought-free, and highly sensory in nature, an awareness in which we experience consciousness extremely clearly. As the biological diminishments of aging demand that we slow down, do one thing at a time, and do it carefully (because rushed, distracted or automatic behavior risks accidents or mistakes we cannot afford), we begin to open up this mystical consciousness often without really being aware of it. We can, on the other hand, experience it directly by intentionally stopping thought, shifting into heightened sensory awareness, and vividly experiencing the world exactly as it is.[24] This is the consciousness of the hunter, mountain climber, or white-water rafter, intensely aware of every detail in the here-and-now. While we already possess this consciousness, we rarely use it. Mystical consciousness naturally opens into Cosmic consciousness, the consciousness of Divinity. We can begin practicing mystical consciousness anytime as we do dishes, move through the house, even talk to others, merging "personal" consciousness with Divinity's pure consciousness.

8. **Experiencing the World as Self.** As the personal self-idea disappears in thought-free mystical consciousness, the rigid boundaries separating us from others and from Divinity grow ever more porous and permeable. As the Hindu greeting *Namaste* implies, the divine in me meets

the divine in you for it is one and the same. From this heightened sense of unity, we realize then that we *are* the world, an experience that profoundly sharpens our morality, for now what happens to others is happening in fact to us. Social justice becomes both personal and spiritual.

9. **Finding Intuitive Understanding of Life, Love, and Divinity.** From the Elder's expanding consciousness flows a radically new understanding of life, yielding a philosophy and spirituality that can be shared with others. The answers to life's great questions are now found far more easily in the intuitions awakened in mystical consciousness, contributing to our transformation into teachers, wisdom figures, and mentors. Like spiritual teachers who embody divine consciousness, we, too, become conduits for Divinity's ongoing revelations.

10. **Shifting from Performing to Unconditional Happiness and Love**. The changes in consciousness described above allow us to cease performing the act of "me" in the world, and discover instead the simple joy of being in flow. Merging consciousness and being creates a natural body-centered joy that effortlessly stirs a naturally spontaneous and love-filled life.

Appendix D. Gifts of Transformed Consciousness

Gifts Received

1. **Comfort.** One of the initial gifts of mystical consciousness is its profound capacity to comfort. No matter what we are feeling, the direct experience of God's consciousness and being as our own brings an incredible relief from stresses and the burdens of everyday life along with a deep atmosphere of serenity and ease. Held in the profound embrace of Divinity, the weary or wounded traveler is rewarded for surrendering the project of self again and again, making everything OK just as it is.

2. **Silence of Mind.** Experiencing the consciousness of Divinity also brings with it a profound silence of mind. There is nothing to think about, question, or figure out. In fact, silence is the doorway to Divinity. Thought, belief, worry and emotion, on the other hand, create the conceptual forms that obscure this spacious and sacred silence. In this silence, moreover, aging no longer exists; we discover instead that the idea of aging is just another complex of thought and belief trapping the thinker in the labyrinth of mind.

3. **Freedom in Flow.** With no more effort expended to be someone, play social roles, or maintain a consistent personality comes exhilarating freedom – from compe- tition, self-improvement, and even the search for meaning. The resulting return to spontaneity allows us to re-enter the flow of being previously suppressed by artificial rules and beliefs. Described as "effortless effort" by Taoism, this flow expresses the divine unfolding of life, and now we are it.

4. **Peace.** Without a false self to wound or defend, there is far less emotional fragility and reactivity, and a far greater capacity for peaceful living. Concern about personal inferiority, failure, self-worth, and the opinions of others disappear. Untroubled by egocentric needs and ambitions, peace opens in the simple confluence of consciousness and being felt in the flow. With no upsets, conflicts, hurt feelings, enemies, or struggles, the personal melodrama of life fades away. As the Buddhists say, "No self, no problem."

5. **Waking Up.** Mystical consciousness shows us just how much we have been living in an artificial world of thought, beliefs, stories, and imagination – literally a dream world comprised of endless illusions and focused on all the wrong things. Enlightenment, to whatever extent it arises, is itself a gift, freeing consciousness for extraordinary new possibilities.

6. **Self as World.** This gift expands the achievement of the previous task of experiencing the world as self. With no self-idea dominating consciousness, the artificial boundaries separating self and other, personal and divine, dissolve into a single reality. We now include or become the other, the world, and all things. We meet the self everywhere as everything. All creation, living or not, is now family, and we no longer feel alone or alienated. Now we enter other living beings, natural processes, and all of existence in new ways evoking transformational understandings, empathy, and love.

7. **A New Center of Consciousness.** Feeling one with Divinity becomes our natural state, for only Divinity remains once thought and the idea of self are gone.

Indeed, God's self is the ultimate gift which becomes our new center of pure and radiant consciousness. Emotion, motivation and behavior transform in this divine awareness, an alchemy changing humanity into Divinity.

8. **Wisdom and Ultimate Knowledge**. There is a kind of intuitive knowing, a gnosis, available in mystical consciousness, showing us how the world really works, the divine nature of the reality, how we create the dream of life, and what "God" really is. Often replacing conventional wisdom or religious beliefs, this kind of knowing is intrinsically convincing and astounding at the same time, providing incredible insights into what used to be insoluble human problems. With this gnosis, we learn that we are already enlightened, already one with God, and already perfect.

9. **Sheer Joy.** The result of all these changes is pure, unconditioned and unmediated joy. As our natural state, joy does not need to be sought, earned, or controlled. Essential to mystical experience, it is, like God, simply what we are made of and always waiting for us to find.

New Gifts to Give

1. **Unconditional Love.** The nature of divine consciousness is unconditional love. We begin to love everyone and everything, and love doing it! This love even goes beyond that known by the initiated Elder for its nature and source is God. The Elder's loving consciousness is infectious, bringing out the natural best in others. Divine love is the gift that replicates itself over and over, healing everything it touches.

2. **Compassion**. Filled with the joy of eternity yet daily confronting people trapped in the worst kinds of ego-created pain evokes deep compassion. A bittersweet gift, it means we must bear others' suffering even as we feel the omnipresent bliss of being. The resulting dissonance intensifies compassion as if insisting that we, too, must be bodhisattvas, for how can there be unity if with any part – no matter how illusory – feels left out?

3. **Increased Capacity for Direct Contact**. Enlightened Elders are naturally and instinctively drawn to direct contact – with kids, adults, animals, plants, sky, earth, everything! - for it is all sacred. Knowledge is valued but only insofar as it leads to real and genuine contact, not for its own sake. Rather than filling consciousness with information, theories, and opinions, fostering the disconnected world of thought, Elders find joy and satisfaction in the direct involvement with life in all its variety and splendor.

4. **New Teaching**. Wherever enlightened Elders go, we are teaching. Consciousness, with its intrinsic gnosis and compassion, offers endless opportunities to demonstrate a new way of life. More important than didactic teaching, this natural illumination spreads from a love-soaked state of being directly in contact with others and is, therefore, powerful beyond words. It is not necessary to be a formal teacher, for now everything we do is a teaching.

5. **New Psychic Capacities**. Those living in the Presence often find themselves blessed with new capacities to heal others through what are more commonly called psychic abilities (known as *charismata* in Christianity or *siddhis* in Hinduism). Enlightened Elders see into the very nature of

things, sense past and future facets of a problem, use energy to heal others, and alleviate the delusions of mind causing suffering.

Appendix E. Preparing for Revelation

1. **Quieting the Mind's Inner Chatter**. After suffering a severe stroke that shut down the verbal left hemisphere of her brain, neuroscientist Jill Bolte Taylor discovered joy, bliss, even Nirvana in the now liberated consciousness of right hemisphere.[25] The perception of Heaven on Earth, she told me, arises in the right hemisphere when the left hemisphere's verbal chatter grows silent [26]– no wonder all the world's religions encourage spiritual practices that quiet the mind. Experiencing the natural quieting inherent in aging expands this same capacity. Whenever we notice unexpected and unexplained joy, we have shifted into chatter-free right hemisphere consciousness.

2. **Living a Slower and More Conscious Life**. As body and mind slow naturally with age, enlightened Elders ease into a more conscious way of life. We move more carefully, reflect longer on the situations before us, and look deeply at life's choices. No longer driven by the rules and reactivity driving the conventional world, we care now about the Earth, life, and all sentient beings. In this expanding mystical consciousness, living grows more precious and holy every day. Instead of reacting to people and events, we move easily, naturally, and spontaneously, like a river flowing around all obstacles. Becoming more patient, we wait to find the path of least resistance around or through problems rather than forcing our will. No longer imprisoned by belief and contraction, our true self expands, assuming its essential and divine nature, and sharing its love and beauty in the world. Now we are the gift, our calm and consciousness awareness opens it, and our life fills effortlessly with new and creative possibilities.

3. **Surrendering Our Obsessive Future Orientation.** As the self-idea and its egocentric motivations disappear from consciousness, so does its future orientation, for in many respects, they are the same thing – a fantasy of how the false self will achieve its goals. Scheduled events, like car maintenance or doctor's appointments, continue but we act without imposing the "project of me" on every situation. When something happens, it's not about me, it's about divine life blossoming like a flower in the mystical consciousness of now. Most remarkably, in this consciousness, the present will always show us the way, what needs doing, and how we can help the world.

4. **Appreciating the Present As It Is.** Sensing time on Earth running out, and indeed time itself dissolving in mystical consciousness, an Elder's appreciation for the gifts of the present moment increases, magnifying its salience, wonder, and value. With only so many sunsets left, we savor the unbelievably beautiful one right before us. We witness the early morning light, our grandson's smile, and our mate's way of brushing her hair. Mystical consciousness changes all it touches, opening our eyes to the Heaven of this world. We begin to understand that the present is all that exists, always and without exception, that enlightenment can only be found here and now, and that this place is divine through and through. Jesus taught that the treasure is here, in this field, right where we are, and we must give up everything to find it. Allah told Muhammad, "I was a buried treasure and I longed to be found, so I created the world so I might be known." The present moment is never boring or unimportant to awakened consciousness; rather it is the treasure chest opening before your eyes.

5. **Living in the Presence.** Pure consciousness, cleansed and always new, awakens the awareness of the divine Presence, for they are one and the same. Commonly experienced as an omnipresent, gentle, intimate, accepting, forgiving, and patient, the experience of Presence melts away contraction and illuminates the beauty and radiance of everyday life. Like washing dirty windowpanes during spring-cleaning, our perception of the world becomes fresh, vivid, amazingly clear, enchanting, and new – dimensions that begin to reveal the beauty of Heaven on Earth everywhere. Learning to experience the Presence not only transforms the Elder's consciousness, it transfigures the world for we are seeing through the eyes of God, opening an extraordinary new dimension to reality. Now the world is alive, radiant with divine consciousness, and pulsing with Divinity.

Appendix F. Changing Our Ideas of Reality

1. **The world is not what you think**. Looking deeply into any object without thought or words, we soon discover that the world beyond thought is infinitely more amazing than anything we can imagine or believe. Stop thinking and see.   ❀

2. **This is the divine world**. All we see here and everything we touch is Divinity. Not the Divinity you think about or imagine, but the One that is all in all. We make this world ugly and frightening with negative thoughts, we make it beautiful by witnessing it in the Presence as Divinity.

3. **Life is a revelation not a problem to be solved**. Divinity constantly reveals its splendor in and as the world, but the mind, with its devaluing, problem-solving agenda, turns everything into problem to be fixed. Realize that revelation is constantly ongoing as the perpetual blossoming of God.

4. **The Universe is conscious and alive**. Divinity saturates everything with its consciousness, including you. Space itself, aware, alive, intimate, holy, and loving, is Divinity holding you and everything in its consciousness.

5. **We are made of God.** Our consciousness and being are the consciousness and being of the Divinity. Experiencing this realization can take us into God, literally, and release torrents of love, joy, and clarity, for pure Being is bliss.

6. **Only God exists, everything else is an illusion**. What relief it is to know that all we fear and believe comprise illusions of mind obscuring infinite being. As contraction,

control, and ego-centered goals dissolve in the thought-free consciousness of Presence, we discover a life beyond your wildest dreams, right here, right now.

7. **Now is all there is.** Past and future do not exist; they are mind forms and fantasies only. It is here that we will find the answers to all our questions and fill all our needs, without moving a single foot.

8. **Enlightenment is happening right now**. Don't look for it elsewhere. Don't imagine how it might be. Enlightenment, cosmic consciousness, Buddha Mind, *satori*, Christ Consciousness, is our essential nature. To remain without thought in the waking state is enlightenment happening.

Appendix G. Gifts of Revelation

Gifts Received

1. **Beauty**. Have you ever watched one of those T.V. specials on the Earth, the ones that bring incredible close-ups of the world's astounding beauty and incredible variety life forms, and thought, "This world is truly amazing!" and then returned to your daily activities without further reflection? Stepping into Heaven on Earth, we discover this same beauty, evoking the same feelings of surprise, awe, reverence, and wonder, except that it's right where we are! And we don't have to go back.

2. **Love.** Like our first romantic swoon, or holding our newborn baby for the first time, experiencing the divine world awakens so much love. This love bursts with praise and gratitude for the extraordinary gift of life in Heaven on Earth. Love also represents our innate response to the Presence, for we instinctively love that which loves everything so generously and unconditionally. Then, at its highest level, we discover that love – unconditional and beyond analysis, is the experience of our own divine nature.

3. **Joy.** Limitless joy pervades Heaven on Earth. In its peace and beauty, we are home, safe, and one with Divinity, and all is well forever and ever. What more could we want? Even more wonderful is the discovery that joy brings more joy. When we are truly, deeply, ecstatically happy, we prime an inner fountain that bubbles with the inherent bliss of being. As the great Hindu mystics taught, bliss erupts from the direct and conscious experience of existence, especially our own being.

4. **Freedom**. To know Heaven on Earth is to be radically and profoundly free. Here, in a consciousness cleansed of thought, there are no boundaries, divisions or limits. Overflowing with love, we need not fear this kind of freedom. Violence and disorder arise from unresolved emotional trauma and destructive beliefs; for the one who has learned to experience Heaven on Earth, freedom means living from awakened perception without hesitation, fear, or self-consciousness.

5. **Community**. In beauty, with love, joy and freedom, we build a new kind of community in Heaven on Earth, one in which all are welcome, encouraged, and loved. When the competition of false selves is finally dissolved, cooperation is pleasure. Like young children who simply love being together, we play in this new community and, in doing so, we contribute to the building Heaven on Earth. And from within this awakened, spirit-based community come new forms of sharing, decision-making, ritual, and celebration.

New Gifts to Give

1. **Beauty.** How can we fail to share the beauty we have found? In sharing the beauty of Heaven on Earth, we invite others to join us there. Beauty itself awakens the perception of the divine world, for in witnessing beauty we are seeing God. As Native Americans have said for centuries, "In beauty, it's begun." And in beauty, we cease viewing the world as an exploitable commodity but as an priceless gift. Who in their right mind would destroy such a gift?

2. **Love**. Love changes people. Patient, kind, forgiving, helpful and loyal, love creates safe and genuine relationships, softening the distrust, rigid defenses, and hard attitudes that keep us apart. In love, the other person matters so much that he or she cannot help but feel special, and in that specialness, wants to love back. It has always been said that love can change the world, and it is true; the problem is that we remain stuck in the fearful and contracted postures of the false self where love quickly becomes conditional and fragile. In Heaven on Earth, love flows from the unlimited nature of our authentic being. What could be easier or more rewarding?

3. **Joy.** Joyful, we naturally share our joy, and it is infectious. Who can remain angry indefinitely at someone who is genuinely happy? In joy, we become a healing presence, showing others that problems are not irresolvable, hurts can be overcome, and life is worth living wherever we are. Joy makes us whole, generous, and grateful. A medicine that constantly replenishes itself, joy is one of the greatest – and easiest – gifts to give.

4. **Freedom.** Freedom is a gift we give to others when we no longer seek to control, direct, or judge them, when we see and bless their true self and encourage its expression. Freedom gives birth to creativity as the inborn energies of this self awaken. As more and more people experience the freedom of Heaven on Earth, things will change quickly and spontaneously. Imagine everyone free to give and receive the gifts of the divine self in this dance of life.

5. **Community.** The community that grows from this dance of loving freedom will change the world. There is enough talent, wisdom, and potential good will in the world to solve all its problems, once we realize who and where we are. A global community built from local communities, sharing resources freely, will become a living entity itself. God will flow through human and non-human systems, until all work together for the whole.

6. **Wisdom**. As we all learn to tap into the wisdom of mystical consciousness, new ideas will create new structures in the world. The building of Heaven on Earth can then begin in earnest. Ideas, rather than being barriers to Divinity, will be expressions of Divinity flowing through individual minds, happily channeling wisdom into community development, architecture, science, the arts, and technology. No longer competitive, this wisdom will lead to a new kind of humanity, one that will exceed all our hopes and dreams.

7. **Awakened Action**. There is a kind of wisdom that comes from *seeing deeply into things as they are.* In this process of intense seeing, a deep knowing emerges spontaneously from reality itself, for we are literally merging with God in this seeing. Focusing intensely on the world as Divinity, we also absorb its divine qualities: compassion, loving-kindness, healing, creativity and wisdom. In this kind of seeing, the enlightened Elder moves from *mystic to prophet,* from one who understands deeply to one who acts on this understanding. We can engage the world with spiritual insight and authority to confront falseness and suffering in all their guises.

Endnotes

1. Robinson, 2009.
2. Jesus, in Meyer, 1992, p. 65.
3. Marharshi, 1984, p. 565.
4. Hanh, 1999, p. 103; 2002, pp. 108-9.
5. Levin, 2002, p. 23.
6. Al-Arabi, in Cjhittick, 1989, p. 379.
7. Firdausi, In Star, 1991, p. 145.
8. Li Po in bly, 1995, p. 247.
9. Seattle, in Mitchell, 1991, p. 176.
10. Tolle, 2005, p 23.
11. Bucke, 1969, p. 156.
12. Goldsmith, 1993, p. 88.
13. Campbell, 1988, p. 230.
14. Chittister, 1999, p. 52.
15. Buddha, in Byrom, 1993, p. 1.
16. deChardin, 1960.
17. Swimme & Berry, 1992.
18. Fox, 1994.
19. Tornstam, 2005.
20. Rimbach, 2010.
21. Ardelt, 2003.
22. Stone, et. Al., 2010.
23. O'Hara, 2010.
24. See Robinson, 2000, for additional instructions.
25. Taylor, 2008.
26. Taylor, personal communication, 2008.

References

Al-Arabi. In Chittick, William. (1989). *The Sufi Path of Knowledge.* NY: State University of New York Press.

Ardelt, Monika. (2003). The Power of Purpose in Aging and Dying Well. Journal of Religious Gerontology, Vol. 14(4) 2003. Retrieved 10/18/10 from http://www.haworthpress.com/store/product.asp?sku=J078 by The Haworth Press, Inc.

Ardagj. Arjuna. (2005). *The Translucent Revolution: How People Just Like You Are Waking Up and Changing the World.* Novato, CA: New World Library.

Bucke, Richard. (1969). *Cosmic Consciousness.* New York: E.P. Dutton and Co.

Byrom, Thomas. (1993). *Dhammapada: The Sayings of Buddha.* Boston: Shambhala Publications.

Campbell, Joseph. (1988). *The Power of Myth.* NY: DoubleDay.

Chardin, Teilhard de. (1960). *The Divine Milieu.* NY: Harper and Row.

Chittister, Joan. (1999). *In Search of Belief.* Miguori, Miss: Liguori/Triumph.

Hanh, Thich. (1999) *Going Home.* NY: Penguin Putnam.

Hanh, Thich. (2002). *No Death, No Fear.* NY: The Berkley Publishing Group.

Firdausi. In Star, Johathan. (Ed.). (1991). *Two Suns Rising.* NY: Bantam Books.

Fox, Matthew. (1994). *The Reinvention of Work.* San Francisco: HarperCollins.

Goldsmith, Joel. (1993). *Conscious Union with God.* NJ: Carol Publishing Group.

Jesus. In Meyer, Marvin. (1992). *Gospel of Thomas.* San Francisco: HarperSanFfancisco.

Levin, Faitel. (2002). *Heaven on Earth.* New York: Kehot Publication Society.

LiPo. In Bly, Robert. (1995). *The Soul Is Here for Its Own Joy*. New Jersey: Ecco Press.

Marharshi, Ramana. (1984). *Talks with Sri Ramana Marharshi*. Tiruvannamalai: Sri Ramanasramam.

Rimbach, Peter. (2010). *Males Coping with Third Age Issues Following Retirement*. Unpublished Doctoral Dissertation, Wisdom University, Mill Valley, CA.

Robinson, John. (1997). *Death of a Hero, Birth of the Soul: Answering the Call of Midlife*. Council Oak Books.

Robinson, John. (2000). *Ordinary Enlightenment: Experiencing God's Presence in Everyday Life*. Unity Village, Mo: Unity House.

Robinson, John. (2009). *Finding Heaven Here*. UK: John Hunt Publishing.

Seattle, Chief. In Mitchell, Stepen (Ed.). (1991). *The Enlightened Mind*. NY: Harper Collins Publishers.

Stone, Arthur, Schwartz, Joseph, Broderick, Joan, Deaton, Angus. (2010). A snapshot of the age distribution of psychological well-being in the United States. Retrieved 10/28/10 from http://www.pnas.org/content/early/2010/05/1003744107.abstract.

Swimme, Brian and Berry, Thomas. (1992). *The Universe Story*. San Francisco: HarperCollins

Taylor, Jill Bolte. (2008). *My Stroke of Insight*. New York: Viking.

Thomas, William. (2007). *What Are Old People For?* Acton, MA: VanderWyk & Burnham.

Tolle, Eckhart. (2005). *A New Earth*. NY: Penguin Group.

Tornstam, Lars. (2005). *Gerotranscendence: A Developmental Theory of Positive Aging*. New York: Springer Publishing Company.

For other information about the work of John C. Robinson, please go to: www. johnrobinson.org.

Other Books by John Robinson

Death of a Hero, Birth of the Soul: Answering the Call of Midlife

But Where Is God? Psychotherapy and the Religious Search

Ordinary Enlightenment: Experiencing God's Presence in
Everyday Life

Finding Heaven Here

B O O K S

O is a symbol of the world, of oneness and unity. In different cultures it also means the "eye," symbolizing knowledge and insight. We aim to publish books that are accessible, constructive and that challenge accepted opinion, both that of academia and the "moral majority."

Our books are available in all good English language bookstores worldwide. If you don't see the book on the shelves ask the bookstore to order it for you, quoting the ISBN number and title. Alternatively you can order online (all major online retail sites carry our titles) or contact the distributor in the relevant country, listed on the copyright page.

See our website **www.o-books.net** for a full list of over 500 titles, growing by 100 a year.

And tune in to myspiritradio.com for our book review radio show, hosted by June-Elleni Laine, where you can listen to the authors discussing their books.